UNRAVELED

The Hope of Coming Undone

SILO CREEK PUBLISHING HOUSE

Unraveled

Copyright © 2019 by Tiffany Bethmann

All rights reserved. No portion of this book may be reproduced, stored in a retrieval system, or transmitted in any form or by any means—electronic, mechanical, photocopy, recording, scanning, or other—except for brief quotations in critical reviews or articles, without the prior written permission of the publisher.

While the author has made every effort to provide accurate internet access at the time of publication, neither the publisher nor the author assumes any responsibilities for errors or for changes that occur after publication. Further, the publisher does not have any control over and does not assume any responsibilities for author or third-party websites or their contents.

Unless otherwise noted, Scripture quotations are taken from The Holy Bible, New International Version ®, NIV®. Copyright © 1973, 1978, 1984, 2011 by Biblica Inc.® Used by permission of Zondervan. All rights reserved worldwide. www.zondervan.com. The "NIV" and "New International Version" are trademarks registered in the United States Patent and Trademark Office by Biblical, Inc. ®

Scripture quotations marked The Message are taken from The Message. Copyright © by Eugene H. Peterson 1993, 1994, 1995, 1996, 2000, 2001, 2002. Used by permission of NavPress. All rights reserved. Represented by Tyndale House Publishers, Inc.

Bible Gateway Translations: https://www.biblegateway.com.

Scripture quotations marked NLT are from New Living Translation © 1996, 2004, 2015 by Tyndale House Foundation.

Scripture quotations marked NKJV are from the New King James Version ©1984 by Thomas Nelson, Inc. Used by permission. All rights reserved.

Any Internet addresses, phone numbers, or company or product information printed in this book are offered as resources and are not intended in any way to be or to imply an endorsement by Silo Creek Publishing House or the author. Neither vouch for the existence, content, or services of these sites, phone numbers, companies, or products beyond the life of this book.

Published by Silo Creek Publishing House / Printed in the United States of America

Silo Creek Publishing House titles may be purchased in bulk for educational, business, fund-raising, or promotional use. For information, please e-mail:
silocreekpublishinghouse@gmail.com.

ISBN: 978-1-7332483-0-3 (paper back)
ISBN: 978-1-7332483-1-0 (ebook)
ISBN: 978-1-7332483-2-7 (audio book)

Library of Congress Control Number: 2019909132

Tiffany is an open, honest, transparent, Christ-following woman who truly lives out surrender to the Holy Spirit. Her book reveals her authentic journey thus far. She invites us to go deeper and to truly know Christ and surrender it all to Him, just as she is trying to do herself. I am so thankful for her invitation to be unraveled.

—Jill Casada

Tiffany Bethmann has written an incredible book for anyone who trusts God to write their story. She teaches us how to stare at God and view life through biblical truth, real life stories, and humor.

—Ashley Goldman, CEO of Evergreen Events

Tiffany has been an inspiration to me since the first time I met her. Her passion for life is contagious, and I'm thrilled that she is sharing her journey with us. Her transparency and vulnerability are humbling and unique. Her story is impactful and moving. I know this book will bless your life as Tiffany has blessed mine!

—Joey Haley, team leader/realtor

YES! YES! YES! Unraveling is not the end! It's only the beginning! In *Unraveled*, Tiffany paints a beautiful picture of the work Jesus Christ does in the hearts and minds of those searching for meaning and purpose. It's a must-read!

—Debbie Williams, Bible study teacher, singer, and pastor's wife

Tiffany brings a real-life approach to the Word of God as she unravels her own life story. Unapologetically herself, Tiffany will make you laugh as you learn about the characters in the Bible and the flaws that ultimately led to their own unraveling. Relatable and raw, *Unraveled* will provide hope to the hopeless by pointing them to prayer.

—Maggie Bailey, mom, wife, and author

Tiffany is passionate about each one of us knowing the Father's heart and how much He truly loves us. She is raw, real, and compassionate as she unravels her journey so that we might open our hearts and allow Him to hold us through our own unraveling. As you walk alongside Tiffany throughout this book, take the time to document your own journey so that you can look back and see how He guided you safely through to the other side.

—**Brooks Reid**, speaker, entrepreneur,
and co-founder of Rolling with the Reids in Franklin, TN

Chaise,

Mom & Dad named you Chaise because of the meaning of your name. "pursuer of Truth" The Bible says God is the way, the Truth + Life.

I pray you always allow God to "unravel" you so you can be used

For my husband, Cort.

For my girls, Rielly, Chaise, and Kailee Grace.

For my parents, Howard and Darla, my sister, Jamie, my niece, Makayla,
my parents-in-law, Bill and Ginger Bethmann, and all my siblings-in-law.

For our stories of chaos, disappointment, and sticking-and-staying.

For all of us looking to God for answers as He unravels us.

May God receive the glory for this crazy little thing called life.

to point others to Jesus!

Love you
Baby Girl

TABLE OF CONTENTS

FOREWORD

I first met Tiffany through a phone call asking for help with unloading their moving truck. Her family had just moved to Franklin, TN from Texas. They were the friends of one of our launch families in our newly-planted church. I made a few calls and a handful of us showed up to lend a hand. As a baby church, we didn't have all the bells and whistles a number of larger, more established churches in the area had. But what we *did* have was heart and hustle. At the end of the day, the Bethmann's chose heart and hustle, and over the last decade, they have been at the point of the spear in our church's maturity and development. We are a better church because of the Bethmann family.

I have personally observed Tiffany live through a portion of God's unraveling and "knitting back" process. Some Sundays, she showed up at church with her arms crossed, not speaking to anyone. It was as if she was fighting against herself to be there. Now, most Sundays she stands in the front row with her arms raised in worship and tears flowing down her cheeks. As you will find in *Unraveled*, the tearing down can be a difficult and sometimes painful process. Many days you are fighting yourself as much as anyone or anything else. But it's worth the struggle.

My first unraveling experience happened when I was 17. I was full of ambition and energy with a varying degree of life aspirations: pilot, engineer, state trooper and baseball player (some dreams die hard!). Oddly enough, it was a knee injury that forced my absence through an entire high school baseball season that sparked my unraveling. I loved Jesus, I loved church. But based on my actions, an outside observer could conclude that I loved baseball more than both.

One evening, I felt particularly sorry for myself and my thigh-to-ankle cast. So I picked up the Bible. I had been repeatedly asking God why this happened to me, and why at this moment, hearing no discernible response from Him. I gave up on the prayer and began reading the Gospel of Matthew. When I got to the end of chapter 6 and read verse 33, it hit me like a cold bucket of water. "Seek first the Kingdom of God and His righteousness and all these things will be added to you."

Void of any answers and at the lowest point of my short life, God met me right there in my bed at the University of Pennsylvania Sports Medicine Center. The verse wasn't merely words on a page—they were energized by the Holy Spirit. I didn't hear a rebuke from God; what I saw was His path forward. I wrote that verse on my cast. My doctor and every nurse had to read that verse and hear my story before I was discharged. Less than one year later—a year of doing everything I could to live Matthew 6:33—I sensed and responded to God's call to ministry!

Almost four decades later, I've learned that unraveling isn't an isolated tool in God's tool box, but a routine process of discipleship. There have been countless other times when God had to "break me down" to build me back up for His ultimate glory.

Unraveling feels counterintuitive to progress. We have been conditioned to interpret forward motion as progress, but if that progress is in the wrong direction, we are just increasing the distance between ourselves and our goal. Check that, if we keep moving in the wrong direction, we are increasing the distance between ourselves and God, the only One who can knit us together again. *Unraveled* will teach you to trust God's process, for most things are better stripped out of our lives than simply patched over.

One of my favorite lines in the book is, "Unraveling isn't fun, but it is not the end of the story." Tiffany is right on both counts! There is a sense of accomplishment in tackling things that are necessary, even though they are not fun. If you can embrace unraveling as part of God's process, you will be able enjoy the unfolding story, even before the last chapter is written.

Life is full of choices. When you picked up this book and decided to embrace it, you made a good choice. If you feel empty, out of options, or at the end of your rope, you have reached the place of hope. Jesus can always be found hanging out in our empty places, ready to remake us in His image.

I pray that Tiffany's transparency and insight light your pathway and help you write your own redemptive story!

Charlie Weir, D.Min.
Founding Pastor
Gateway Franklin Church
www.gatewayfranklin.com

THE NEED FOR UNRAVELING

Tears of disbelief streamed down my face as I pulled into the parking lot of Walgreens. I quickly purchased a pregnancy test that would determine whether the impossible had occurred. *This could never happen to me.* I was convinced of it.

Sure enough, those two pink lines stared back at me, seemingly as shocked as I was. *What have I done?*

To this day, those lines are etched in my memory, paving a road of sorrow.

I felt so alone. The darkness in my heart and the numbness in my mind tore me apart. I longed for comfort. Anger ran through my veins. I felt like I was cast out in the cold with only the whispers of condemnation blowing through my mind.

I had my whole life ahead of me. I was going to do great things. And now, all those dreams would be thrown in the garbage along with my reputation. I had all the hormones of a teenager plus the raging emotions of a pregnant lady. How could I, a sixteen-year-old with a broken brain, have a child? How could I provide for and raise a responsible adult when I can't even vote? How could I weather this storm?

As my mind and heart dove deeper into despair, I cried out to God with the only prayer I could muster. "God, I know You said I'm not alone. But I feel like I am shipwrecked, a castaway."

The decisions I faced over the next several months were some of the scariest of my life. During that pregnancy, God gently led me and unraveled me for His glory. My life forever changed course the day those two pink lines appeared. Those lines represented the beginning of my messy, beautiful unraveling.

We All Unravel

To unravel is "to disengage or separate the threads of, to disentangle; to cause to come apart by or as if by separating the threads of, to resolve the intricacy, the complexity, or the obscurity of; to clear up."[1]

I don't know about you, but I have asked God for clarity so many times in life. I've needed Him to clear up some of the crazy complexities and absurdities of life so that I could come to a mental resolve as to why I had to endure hardship.

We are masters of appearances and failures of honesty.

The way "unravel" has defined itself in my life is the very reason I felt lead to share this book, this study, with others. Because I've been there, I knew I could help answer the big questions we ask: "Why, God? Why me? Isn't there an easier way?"

Even deeper, I know what it's like to ask the bigger, scarier questions like, "If You love me, why are You allowing these things to happen to me?"

I see unraveling as coming to the end of ourselves and meeting God there. It's a simple definition, one that's easier said than done. The *problem* with this concept of unraveling is simple, too. We just don't want to. We live in a world and culture where we desire comfort to the point that we will do whatever it takes to achieve it. We want to be known and loved; at the same time, we cover and mask the underlying truth about ourselves.

Deep down, we are all uncomfortable. We try to camouflage our messy lives by looking and appearing as though we fit right in. We go on fancy trips, partake in dirty pleasures, indulge in food and drink, and adopt culturally-popular traps. We are masters of appearances and failures of honesty. We hustle to present our lives as though we have it all together, with facades that look and feel impressive on the surface. However, before we can truly have a beautifully-woven life, we must allow God to unravel us. We have to allow God to undo us in order to remake us, to deconstruct us in order to rebuild us.

Most of us are all about the second half of that story. We'd love to be remade and rebuilt, to be better than before. But we want to take the shortcut and push the easy button. We are a society with a "my way, right away" mentality. But that isn't how things happen in God's society. We can't leap frog our way to the end. The journey, the bumps, the stumbles— these are all part of the unraveling process. This is what it takes to form us into the person God created us to be.

Unraveling Isn't Fun, But It's Not the End of the Story

Buckle up for this ride. Unraveling is a journey. While you might not see the end right now—only the darkness around you—rest assured that God is in the exchange business. God might be asking us to remove something, someone, an idea, a long-held way of doing things, or a comfortable pattern. Quite frankly, this isn't fun. However, when we choose to allow God to unravel what we know, and allow Him to reveal the new? *That* is living the high life!

I'm not going to lie to you. If you're anything like me, when you face hardships and trials, you might have moments when you feel like the game has come to an end. There is no surviving. You're going under. This is it. That may be the song you are singing today, but it isn't the song you will continue to sing for long. How do I know that to be true?

The basic theology of the Bible is a tear-down-and-build-up principle. God tore down the junk that Israel built. The Old Testament is filled with accounts of Israel's persistent disobedience. Psalm 78:10-11 mentions that Israel did not keep the covenant of God. They chose to do it their way instead of God's way. Time and time again in the Book of Exodus, the Israelites forgot they served a powerful God, even after God miraculously saved them. It was a painful process for them, yet the pain lead to the process of the remaking and rebirthing of a Kingdom that will not be destroyed.

It is throughout the unraveling process that God transforms us and reveals our story, our identity. He gives us a voice to share. We are to spread the love and grace of our Heavenly Father to our arenas, our people, and our areas of influence.

"And we know that in all things God works for the good of those who love him, who have been called according to his purpose." –Roman 8:28

As we move through the adventure of allowing God to unravel us, my prayer is that we will hold fast to Romans 8:28. Life is going to throw us a lot of, "What the heck?!" moments. We need to remind ourselves that God is going to use every single one of these moments for good because He brings about good for those who love Him.

In the end, these overwhelmingly difficult hardships, pains, and trials will be instrumental in showing us our purpose, the story God has already written for us. And we will tell a story that brings glory to God and hope to His people.

A Position to Begin

Let's position ourselves mentally and physically to understand. To position ourselves mentally and physically to understand involves getting to a place where we no longer have willpower to fight or decipher things on our own. We have to let go of the fantasies of running away and release the desire to know what is to come. Let's stop searching for the answers and just quietly wait. There's nothing weak or passive about that.

My friend, Trina, was given no hope of surviving her brain surgery. She was instructed to say goodbye to her kids and family. She was brought to her knees; she had no choice but to let it be and let God be God. She let God be the Lord of her situation because she physically didn't have the ability to fight. So she surrendered.

When we get to the end of ourselves, we get to God. We reach the moment of being stripped down and prepared for remodeling. When life challenges, unravels us, to the point of breaking, it is then that we will truly discover our purpose and embrace life in the middle of our mess. And it is here that Christ is glorified.

That's what Trina did. And God unraveled her. But He also brought her through that surgery, giving her more time to share about His goodness.

God Sees the Final Picture

Why does it seem that some people get away with murder and are blessed? While others, like myself, feel like their life is a wreck?

I once heard Priscilla Shirer explain why it looks like some people live the good life without issue, correction, or suffering, while others get caught at the slightest wrong. She told the story of a child she once saw in a store. The child was being rude and disrespectful to her mom. As the child was yelling and causing a scene, other shoppers couldn't help but glance at the disruptive, disrespectful behavior. Good southern mommas have the instinct to think, "Poor thing, I have been there. But darling, you better do something about that quick. The little hot mess you're dealing with now is definitely going to be to hard to handle in a couple of years!"

That might seem judgmental, but every mom has had to face this fact and decide how they are going to handle their little munchkin's meltdowns. It's a (difficult, challenging, tear-inducing) responsibility of parenting.

What if God views things this way? What if some people don't get the correction from God because, well, they haven't made Him the Lord of their life? Have you ever thought of that? Maybe I am instructed and lovingly disciplined because my Creator cares for me. He cares to take time to correct me, unravel me, and change me because He's deeply invested in the person I'm becoming. Just like we are with our children.

Teaching my child the tough lessons in life is much more important than their comfort right now. I parent for the long haul. So does God. I imagine He doesn't enjoy those seasons of unraveling in our lives, just like discipling our kids is one of the most difficult aspects of parenting. But, just like us, God is working toward the final picture.

Finding the Honey

In the days of parenting littles, I discovered that my kids loved honey sticks. They would act like Saint Peter greeting people at heaven's door in order to gain this reward. It became a life-changer. Scratch that, a life-*saver*.

Before a trip to the grocery store, I would say, "Girls, if you mind your manners, play pretty, and obey at the checkout, I will reward you with a honey stick." It only cost me twenty-five cents a piece. It was the most useful seventy-five cents in our budget!

Even to this day, at the ages of 20, 15, and 13, any time we are in the grocery store, my precious girls say, "If I mind my manners, can I get a honey stick?"

Repetition is part of unraveling. We learn by repeating. Those sweet honey sticks became a weekly routine by which change occurred. Once we taste the sweetness of what God is teaching us and doing in our lives, we are more open to the next phase. The sweetness attracts us, and we imagine how sweet the end will taste. Training Miss Independent Spirit to become Miss Dependent on God is a hard, slow process. But in the end, it is worth it.

Are You Ready to Unravel?

Henry T. Blackaby said, "When you know what God has said, know what He is about to do and have adjusted your life to Him, there is yet one remaining necessary response to God. To experience Him at work in and through you, you must obey Him. When you obey Him, He will accomplish His work through you, and you will come to know Him by experience."[2]

Are you ready for the experience? Some of us will be, others not so much (I'm often standing with the latter).

I grew up in a Christian home with a loving family. I love my family, but there have been several times in life when I've asked God why on earth He put me in such a crazy, dysfunctional mess. We are loud and proud people. We can accomplish anything we put our minds to; we are talented and determined. Growing up, I was surrounded by cousins, aunts, uncles, and grandparents. While we all have a little dysfunction in our families, mine puts the *fun* in dysfunctional. We party big, eat like we are Greek, and fight like we are in the Mafia.

Despite all the mess, I wouldn't trade my place in my family for anything. My experiences, my talents, my flaws, and my blessings all resulted from God placing me exactly where I needed to be.

Our society often tells us that when life throws us curveballs, we become helpless victims. Well, that is the biggest bunch of poppy-cock I have ever heard. We may not have control over our circumstances, but we absolutely have control over how we respond. We can react the way God's Word tells us, or we can try it our own way until we come to the end of our rope, throw our hands up, and say, "Lord, help me! I need You!"

The Bible is full of stories of the men and women who persevered through life, striving to seek out and obey the will of God in hopes of receiving the promise of God. Most of them didn't get the results they wanted in their lifetimes. When we begin to allow the Lord to unravel us, we begin to understand what it truly means to hope for the fulfillment of God's promises. We see this unfold in the lives of God's faithful ones like Jacob, Abraham, and David. Each of them tried to handle life on his own, without

God. And each ultimately allowed God to unravel him to the point that he realized to truly be independent, he must be dependent on God.

If I would have allowed my girls to act like crazy monkeys in the grocery instead of insisting on manners and discipline, they would have had a harder time becoming independent. Yet through their dependency on *us*, they took steps toward becoming strong girls who are able to think for themselves. Our boundaries and guidance actually made them more free.

Real freedom comes from being dependent on God. Life is hard. Life is messy. But unraveling with Christ brings unimaginable beauty from even the most hopeless ashes.

Real freedom comes from being dependent on God.

How to Read This Book

There is no single right way to read this book, friend. It can be read alone, with a friend, or in a small group.

This book is divided into six parts. You could read it like a six-week study. If you choose to read it rhythmically, you will read each part's introduction on Sunday, and one chapter each day on Monday-Friday.

Ultimately, this book is flexible, just like our hearts should be during the unraveling process. Do what works for you! Allow the Holy Spirit to direct your reading as you open your heart to His movements.

Part One

UNRAVELING TO BELIEVE

"Trust in the Lord with all your heart and lean not on your own understanding; in all your ways submit to him, and he will make your path straight." —Proverbs 3:5-6

This verse has been a cornerstone in my life. When I read it, I shake my head in awe of the awesomeness of God. It's also a verse that is easier to speak than to live.

In 2007, I became overwhelmed by what I felt where my shortcomings. God was moving my family into a new season. I had been a stay-at-home mom to three beautiful girls while my husband worked full-time and attended school full-time. We sensed a change in our season.

My husband, Cort, had finished his undergraduate degree and felt led to law school. As if that wouldn't be enough change, God led us to leave the comforts of our home in Tennessee and move to Texas. We were scared to death, yet we had peace. How is it possible to be scared and have peace at

While we might not know how it all ends, we know that God is faithful and His Word is trustworthy.

the same time? When you put your trust in the character of God. When you trust someone, you are able to find harmony in what seems like contradiction by relying on their track record. If they did it before, they will do it again. While we might not know how it all ends, we know that God is faithful and His Word is trustworthy.

This kind of confidence takes time to build. It did for us when God put this call on our lives. We basically had two weeks of pay in our pockets, a stack of resumes, and no clue how it would all turn out. I will never forget the 4th of July we moved to Texas. My husband looked at me and said, "Are you going to be able to do this?" I returned his stare and said confidently, "Absolutely! I can do this!"

Honestly, I was giving myself a pep talk. I would need it. During our first week in Texas, I sat in my minivan in a foreign parking lot and prayed, "God, You have to do this!" I reminded myself of Proverbs 3:5-6.

Confessing beyond what I could see, I reminded myself that I needed to trust God. I prayed, "God, You brought us out here. My family, my babies, my husband—everyone is counting on me. I feel this unbelievable weight on my shoulders. Please, give me the confidence and favor to do what You have called me to do. Help me to rely on Your ways and not my feelings. Remove my way of thinking and unravel my thought process so I can learn to depend on You alone."

I got out of my car and walked through the doors of different businesses. I introduced myself and asked if they were hiring. No matter their answer, I would finish by pitching myself to the managers. I told them why I would be the best employee. By the end of that week, even though I had not worked for severals years, I was offered a job. I went from full-time mom to full-time provider.

At this time, I only had two years of college under my belt. The jump from that reality to the reality of having several job offers, making more than what we made in our old town, proves how important belief is in the unraveling process. I believed that God could take my unqualified, uneducated self and allow me to help my family not only survive, but thrive.

Where in your life do you need the Proverbs 3:5-6 mindset? Where do you need to trust the Lord with all your heart, leaning not on your own thoughts, feelings, or understandings? Where do you need to submit to Him, knowing that He will make your path straight?

Take time to jot down or think through Proverbs 3:5-6. Apply it to your life right now and what you are going through. Rewrite the Scripture into your own words.

We all experience times when we struggle to believe what God says is true, especially when nothing around us points to security. In this section, we will dive into the lives of some powerful women in Scripture. Let's see what we can learn from their stories and how God can teach us some major truths through the unraveling of their lives.

Let Us Pray

Lord, I know You are with me at all times. Nothing surprises You or catches You off guard. I refuse to be a Bitter Betty. I know the enemy can't take me out, but Satan is trying to wear me out. Help me, Lord! Please help Your truth to resonate in my mind and heart. This trial doesn't define my life. Not even this has thrown a kink in Your plan for me.

Make my mind like a sponge, soaking in the promise that You see me. You aren't going to let my foot slip; You will use this for Your glory! Give me discernment and direction as I learn to walk in this season of unraveling. I love You, Lord! You are awesome! Thank You for loving me and holding me up. Let all this be done in the precious Name of Jesus. Amen.

Chapter 1

BEING IN THE KNOW

One of the best things God has called me to is being the mom of three amazing daughters, Rielly, Chaise, and Kailee Grace. God equipped all three with incredible personalities and different traits and desires. Watching them grow and experiencing life with them has been such a precious gift from God.

With our first daughter, going through high school was very scary. Not just for her, but for us as well. We died on some of those mountains that didn't need to be died on. Quite frankly, we thought we were in the know, but later found out we were so far out of the loop.

We are no longer "rookie parents" when it comes to high school. We have learned a thing or two from raising our oldest. For example, the task of choosing high school courses. High school is so different from when we were in school. They ask kids to select a field and declare a major by their junior year. I don't know who came up with this idea, but whoever did probably never raised a child. Asking these kids to declare a major is overwhelming. I mean, just observe a Sonic drive through with a car full of teenagers. For them, choosing a slushie or shake flavor is like deciding whether or not to drop another atomic bomb. The thought of planning their lives, and all the what-if's they entail, seriously freaks them out.

Despite my distaste of this approach, we try to reassure our children that it is completely normal to be unsure college majors. Even in college, most people change majors. We remind them that they don't need to know every detail of how it is all going to work out.

Planner People

For people who love to plan, chart, and create spreadsheets, being in the know is a breath of fresh air. If left to my comforts, the song I would perpetually sing would be "Let it Be" by The Beatles. However, since most of my friends like to plan, I have learned to do my best to plan in hopes of relieving any anxiety they might feel when they don't know the plan.

I think Eve might have been the planner in her marriage. She liked knowing the details, being an "in-the-know" kind of person. I think Adam might have been a "go-with-the-flow" kind of dude. That's my assumption after seeing how things played out for them in the Garden of Eden.

Let's dive into Genesis 3 and see what we can learn from how Eve handled her encounter with the serpent (the devil) on the day that changed the world.

"Now the serpent was more crafty than any of the wild animals the Lord God had made. He said to the woman, "Did God really say, 'You must not eat from any tree in the garden'?""—Genesis 3:1

This verse illustrates the serpent's attempt to cause Eve to doubt God. Where, in your life, is the serpent trying to stir up doubt in your heart?

"The woman said to the serpent, "We may eat fruit from the trees in the garden, but God did say, 'You must not eat fruit from the tree that is in the middle of the garden, and you must not touch it, or you will die.'" "You will not surely die," the serpent said to the woman. "For God knows that when you eat from it your eyes will be opened, and you will be like God, knowing good and evil.""—Genesis 3:2-4

When I read that, I can't help but think about my own life. The enticement to be like others, to have what they have, pulls me in. When I walk through hardships or trials, I start running through the how's and why's in my mind. I try to figure out what I am missing. Heck, it doesn't even have to be a hardship. It can simply be learning about a new gadget or a new legging brand whose prices equal half a car payment.

It makes no sense, yet we fall prey to the desire to be included and to have the new thing. I allow my feelings, my heart, and my emotions to take over. I have even allowed others to convince me of what *they* think. I have allowed them to deceive me with flattery and with the prospect of gaining power. I would have eaten the apple, because I would have wanted to see everything for myself. I would want to make sure I wasn't missing out. I would want to be in the know.

"When the woman saw that the fruit of the tree was good for food and pleasing to the eye, and also desirable for gaining wisdom, she took some and ate it. She also gave some to her husband, who was with her, and he ate it. Then the eyes of both of them were opened, and they realized they were naked; so they sewed fig leaves together and made coverings for themselves." –Genesis 3:6-7

If we look at how the serpent enticed Eve, we gain great insight. The serpent tempted Eve with a half-truth. The half-truth was that their eyes would be opened. But they never see with the eyes and mind of God.

"Then the man and his wife heard the sound of the Lord God as he was walking in the garden in the cool of the day, and they hid from the Lord God among the trees of the garden. But the Lord God called to the man, "Where are you?" He answered, "I heard you in the garden, and I was afraid because I was naked; so I hid." And he said, "Who told you that you were naked? Have you eaten from the tree that I commanded you not to eat from?" The man said, "The woman you put here with me—she gave me some fruit from the tree, and I ate it." Then the Lord God said to the woman, "What is this you have done?" The woman said, "The serpent deceived me, and I ate."" –Genesis 3: 8-13

We Have His Promise

One advantage we have over Eve is the Bible. This is a *huge* advantage. We have Scripture. We have an instruction book of guidelines. We get to learn from those who went before us, from those who wanted to be in the know. When we face big decisions, the Bible should be our map. When we use it correctly and go to it to seek an answer, it guides us and directs us. Clear answers might not come immediately, but the Word is a promise from the Lord.

"Your word is a lamp unto my feet, and a light for my path." –*Psalm 119:105*

We can rest in knowing that when we seek an answer, we will surely find it.

Take a moment and rewrite God's promise to you in your own words.

What are you currently facing in life that needs the light of this truth?

The Book of Proverbs is packed with verses about avoiding hasty, quick decisions and instructions on how to make wise decisions. Eve made a knee-jerk decision in the heat of the moment because she wanted to be in the know. In reality, sometimes God leaves us out of the loop so that we don't become paralyzed with fear. Otherwise, we might become overwhelmed by what He has called us to do. Just as He unravels us slowly, He reveals to us when to move and when to stop because He understands just how much we can handle.

So while we desire the details, old wives' wisdom tells us: the devil is in the details.

Run to the Throne

I think it is unwise for schools to force our kids in high school to make decisions that they aren't ready to handle yet. Realistically, they don't need to know everything. Just like Eve, we have free will. Free will to choose. Choose this day whom you will serve, and what choices you will make, and what path you will take. It is a daily choice. I choose to serve God by trusting, even though I can't see His plans. I choose to trust God—not myself—to make a wise choice.

It seems silly, but all too often, we run to friends and other sources to find wisdom instead of running to God and His Word for guidance. We all enjoy feeling like a part of something; hence, our churches, schools, and work places are filled with gossip. And we are eager to add to it. It's why we kill ourselves, slaving away at our jobs just to get those initials behind our name. It's why we aim to be the PTO president as school. We crave power and the knowledge instead of trust and surrender.

Let's pause and refocus. Let's ask God to be our eyes, to guide us through His Word instead of following our feelings and our friend's ideas.

What specific situation are you facing? What decision are your struggling to make? Maybe it's a temptation to be in the know. I journaled the prayer below when I was facing one of those moments in my life. I desperately didn't want to miss the will of God or fall into the trap Eve did. I wanted to learn from her "unraveling moment." I wanted God to unravel me and remake my way of approaching life and decisions.

Take a moment and pray this specific prayer over what you are facing. Allow God to unravel your way of thinking and pour new truths into your heart to guide you.

Let Us Pray

Lord, before I make this decision (________________________________), I choose to seek Your Word for the answer. I choose to pause and spend time allowing Your Word to unfold itself and guide me. I want Your peace and power to guide me, not my feelings or emotions, which can deceive me. Forgive me for the times I've run to my phone instead of Your throne, or when I trusted myself without seeking Your Word for insight and truth. Bless me indeed, O Lord! Guide me and protect me from evil. Amen.

Forgive me for the times I've run to my phone instead of Your throne.

Chapter 2

ARE YOU KIDDING ME?

Have you ever been in a situation that went from bad to worse?

I'm talking about the situations you experience in a hospital waiting room. Moments you stare aimlessly at the dull, gray walls, the news blaring from the TV with the day's depressing headlines. You're stuck waiting, watching helplessly in the ICU, hoping against all odds that the doctor's predictions are wrong. Maybe you have experienced a time when the doctor, donning scrubs and puffy eyes, walks into the waiting room and tells you that they aren't certain what is wrong with the person you love. You stay suspended in disbelief that these experts have no answers for you. No projection of what the road to recovery looks like. Their only answer is "more tests," which tests your spirit of patience.

Or maybe your bad-to-worse moments look different. You have served your company faithfully for 20 years. One day, you're called in to the office, and everything you have known is swept away with the wave of a pink slip. Your position has been terminated, and you have two weeks to find a new job.

Maybe you receive a phone call that knocks the very breath out of you. The voice on the other end informs you that your loved one has been in a car wreck. You need you to identify the body.

Maybe the spouse you love with all your heart, the one you have faithfully slept beside every night despite the opportunities to be unfaithful, keeps pulling away from you. There is no sign of change. You mumble to your lonely self, "Are you kidding me?" No matter how hard you try, you seemed to have lost that loving feeling.

Maybe you have faithfully asked God to bring you your Prince Charming. Yet with every passing day, you can't shake the feeling that you may never get your happily ever after.

Maybe you're stuck in a job you absolutely hate. You've applied to other jobs and have jumped through the interview hoops. But they always seem to choose someone else over you. You wonder why you're being passed over, time and time again.

These situations leave us breathless and doubtful. We become so frustrated by our failed attempts. We say, "Are you kidding me?" as if to express a loss of hope. If you have been there, or if you're in the middle of the impossible, you're not alone. Don't believe the lie that God can't do it, will not do it, or that it is just too big or too far gone. I have had my fair share of "impossibles," when all I can do is question God. I am sure I will have more!

You Did Laugh

In the Bible, Sarah has one of these, "Are you kidding me?" moments. It is so insightful to see how God used her situation that seemed impossible, even ridiculous, to unravel her and remake her. Let's see how Sarah handled it.

"The Lord appeared again to Abraham near the oak grove belonging to Mamre. One day Abraham was sitting at the entrance to his tent during the hottest part of the day. He looked up and noticed three men standing nearby. When he saw them, he ran to meet them and welcomed them, bowing low to the ground." –Genesis 18:18

The Bible tells us that the Lord appeared again to Abraham, and yet when he looked up he noticed three men. This was likely Jesus and two angels. God knew He was going to come through, even if Abraham and Sarah thought nothing was going to change on this hot day. God was making good on His promise, despite how Sarah and Abraham both doubted and took matters into their own hands.

""My lord," he said, "if it pleases you, stop here for a while. Rest in the shade of this tree while water is brought to wash your feet. And since you've honored your servant with this visit, let me prepare some food to refresh you before you continue on your journey." "All right," they said. "Do as you have said." So Abraham ran back to the tent and said to Sarah, "Hurry! Get three large measures of your best flour, knead it into dough, and bake some bread." Then Abraham ran out to the herd and chose a tender calf and gave it to his servant, who quickly prepared it. When the food was ready, Abraham took some yogurt and milk and the roasted meat, and he served it to the men. As they ate, Abraham waited on them in the shade of the trees." –Genesis 18:3-5 (NLT)

I love this next verse. God is so good at asking questions, as if He doesn't already know the answers.

""Where is Sarah, your wife?" they asked him. "There in the tent," he said. Then the Lord said, "I will surely return to you about this time next year, and Sarah your wife will have a son!"" –Genesis 18:8-10

Sarah was listening to this conversation from the tent. I am sure she was very interested in what the messengers had to say, so she eavesdropped.

Abraham and Sarah were both very old at this time, and Sarah was long past the age of having children. So she laughed and said to herself:

""How could a worn-out woman like me enjoy such pleasure, especially when my master—my husband—is also so old? Then the Lord said to Abraham, "Why did Sarah laugh? Why did she say, 'Can an old woman like me have a baby?' Is anything too hard for the Lord? I will return about this time next year, and Sarah will have a son." Sarah was afraid, so she denied it, saying, "I didn't laugh." But the Lord said, "No, you did laugh." –Genesis 18:11-15 (NLT)

I can't help but notice that Sarah's impossible situation had a flair for a modern-day reality show gone wrong. It makes me laugh a little. Imagine it! We have a lady who would have been on Medicare, trying to get into a skilled nursing facility, and God's messengers roll up and say, "You are going to have a son!"

Don't even act like you wouldn't laugh, too. Some of us might even drop some four-letter words. Think about the "birthing center" in which she would have this precious, chosen child. It would be in the middle of nowhere, without pain meds, without sitz baths. And it would all go down in a tent in the middle of the desert without air conditioning. Forget laughing, I would have lost my cool right there!

Sometimes, God presents us with impossible situations as an invitation to unravel so that He can make us into what He has created and destined us to become.

What situation are you currently facing that might seem impossible for you to the point of laughter or anger?

We also learn that Sarah got off track when she desperately tried to "help" God keep His promise. Sarah's timing and God's timing didn't coincide. Sarah felt that *not* having her son right away signaled a delay. So she decided to take matters into her own hands. She came up with a plan about how God's promise "should" be fulfilled.

Sarah prompted her husband to sleep with her servant, Hagar. Not only did she delay the promise, but she complicated the process. I am 100% guilty of trying to make sense of God's promise and taking matters into my own hands. But like Sarah, every time I do, I look up only to witness the utter mess I've made.

As we think about Sarah and how she took matters into her own hands, stop and think about *your* impossible situation. How might you be trying to take matters into your own hands? How are you trusting in yourself more than you're trusting in God?

Write a prayer asking God to forgive you for elevating yourself to His level and thinking that you could ever make something happen without Him. Confess to God how you desperately need Him to show you how He is the God of the impossible and that He is the One who sits on the throne.

Just the Beginning

Get ready for it. This is just the beginning of a beautiful thing. It might not feel amazing right now, but prepare yourself. Here comes the unraveling.

I believe God is looking into our hearts to see what lies within because He is always interested in our growth. God uses what we are going through for our good.

During times when we are steeped in the impossible, we have to be willing to get real with God. We need to speak with Him from our hearts instead of giving the textbook, "right" answers. We have to dig deeper in the unraveling and allow our head knowledge to sink to our hearts. We have to get real with ourselves, and we have to be honest before God. We aren't kidding God. He is omniscient. That means that He not only sees our true colors and character, but He knows what we think and what we plan. So don't give Him lip service. Get real. If we want to have faith that moves mountains, we must allow His truth to capture our hearts.

First, we need to look back and recall what God has done for us in the past. Stop right now and name three times He showed up and was faithful to you:

In the above examples, did you think this was how God was going to work it out? Reflect below.

If He has done it before, He will do it again! The journey may not look the way we want it to look or fit within our time frame, but He is the same God yesterday, today, and tomorrow.

Take a moment to reflect on the Scripture verses below. I encourage you to memorize them, or write them out on index cards and carry them in your purse. You might feel like this is juvenile or pointless, but there's nothing pointless about hiding the Word in our hearts and minds. When we face unraveling, we have truth to stand on when we face fear, anger, or shame.

"Know therefore that the LORD your God is God, he is the faithful God, keeping His covenant of love to a thousand generations of those who love Him and keep His commandments." –Deuteronomy 7:9

"If we are faithless, He remains faithful, for He cannot disown Himself." –2 Timothy 2:13

"For the Word of the Lord is right, and true; he is faithful in all He does." –Psalm 33:4

"But the Lord is faithful, and He will strengthen and protect you from the evil one." –2 Thessalonians 3:3

The only way to allow our faith to grow and to be able to trust God with the impossible is to understand God's character. There is no other way to learn the character of God than by learning what God's Word says to be true, and then doing life with God. When we can begin to put to memory the above verses and truly learn them, we grasp the character of God. When we can understand His character, then we can boldly trust God with our impossibles instead of leaning on our own understandings, feelings, or thoughts. We can face the impossible, our doubt in God's promises, or even those moments when we try to take matters into our own hands, simply by trusting Him more deeply.

Let Us Pray

Lord, help me to get real with myself. Help me to be honest before You, because You know what truly lies in my heart. Help me to remove the lip service. Help me to believe firmly in Your character. Help me understand that, while I feel like I have hit rock bottom, You are the Rock of my life. Help me to realize that these verses take time to heal and transform my heart. Help me to stay diligent as You rebuild my thought process through Your Word. Show me that You are worthy of my trust. Give me a longing and desire in my heart to hunger for Your Word.

Chapter 3

FEELING TRAPPED? GOD WILL MAKE A WAY

I despise carnations. Early on in our relationship, I emphasized to my husband that he was to *never* purchase me carnations in any shape, color, or form. I don't even like them as fillers in other flower arrangements. I refer to them as the "funeral flower."

On Broadway, if an actor gets fired, their superiors give them a send-off flower. Do you know what that flower is? That's right, the dreaded carnation. The "we will see you later" flower. The "you're dead to us now" flower.

However, recently I strolled past the floral department in my grocery store. I heard a whisper in my heart, compelling me to buy a bouquet of pink carnations. I wrestled with the very idea that I was even thinking of purchasing carnations. How would I ever live this down with my family? I tried to talk myself into the other gorgeous spring flowers, but I couldn't stop my eyes from darting back to the pink carnations. So I bought them.

As I wheeled my grocery cart out of the store and toward my car, I thought to myself, "Yep, this is it. You have gone off the deep end. You bought the funeral flowers instead of the exquisite spring bouquet with the vibrant splashes of colors."

"I'll never forget you."

I still didn't understand what drew me to purchase the pink carnations. But the answer became clear later that evening. During my quiet time with God, I was inspired to research what the color of pink carnations symbolizes. To my surprise and amazement, the meaning of those ugly, death-signifying flowers is: *'I'll never forget you.*

No matter what we face, we can rest assured that God will never forget us! He sees exactly where we are and where we are going.

God unravels the way we think. He unravels our assumptions and compulsions. And He does it in ways we would never imagine. Who would have predicted that God would use the flower I hated the most to reveal His love to me that day? He used what I avoided to tell me that He never avoids me, that He sees me.

Hagar's Unraveling

Sometimes our unraveling occurs because of others and the decisions they make. Others make impulsive decisions that cost us dearly, and we don't deserve to have to walk through these moments of unraveling. Someone might be so convinced that they know what is best, or that their gut is telling them something, and so they betray our trust and our love.

When Hagar became pregnant by Abraham (at Sarah's request), she gave him a son. Suddenly, Sarah didn't like the way she was treated by Hagar. Sarah became jealous and angry, and demanded that Abraham dismiss her maidservant and her child from the camp.

Hagar experienced her own unraveling. Hagar felt used, abused, and mistreated. She did the only thing she could think to do: she ran. The odds weren't in her favor. She was a servant woman in a foreign land. She was alone in the desert. But the Lord found her.

Have you ever experienced a hardship or trial when you felt stuck because you had no idea how to fix it?

I feel this way weekly, if not daily.

Has someone made a decision that impacted your life without first consulting you? What emotions did it stir up in your heart?

When someone makes a decision involving me without first consulting me, it usually brings up fear. I feel that they no longer need me. I feel rejected and abandoned. This usually manifests as anger. Of course, once I have an outburst, I usually feel even worse 30 minutes later. I take the bait from Satan.

Have you ever felt trapped? Have you felt overlooked in matters that are important to your life? Have you ever felt like God forgot you? Are you living through that right now? Write about the experience and the emotions you feel/felt.

God Never Wills Your Abuse

Just as Hagar faced horrible injustice, we face similar trials in life. When we are faced with having to walk through a trial due to others' choices, it can cause us to question if God even sees us. This wound is especially deep if the person seems to skate along without any consequences.

I want to pause for a moment and address the elephant in the room. God never intends for you to be abused. God takes what Satan means for evil— the very thing that Satan thought would kill you, steal you, or destroy you— and He uses it for good.

Disturbing and detrimental situations like these cause us pain, bitterness, anger, shame, fear, and frustration. However, when we chose to allow God to unravel our thinking and reframe it as a kingdom perspective, we can face hardships with confidence based on God's Word.

And we know that in all things God works for the good of those who love him, who have been called according to his purpose. –Romans 8:28

You intended to harm me, but God intended it for good to accomplish what is now being done, the saving of many lives. –Genesis 50: 20

Abuse is never willed by God. It is never good. No one should live through it. However, I do think it is absolutely beautiful when God takes someone's painful story and allows the abuse that should have destroyed them to unravel them and reveal a purpose through the pain. Their story of healing and the overwhelming obstacles they overcame can help others overcome and have the confidence to receive freedom.

If you have experienced any type of abuse, I encourage you to seek professional healing. Talk to a trusted individual, or contact an abuse hotline.[1] If you are experiencing those types of injustices, you need someone to walk beside you through the valley. A trained professional can be your companion on your road to healing and restoration.

Calling Out the Lies

You don't have to have experienced the horror of abuse to experience the same emotions Hagar felt.

Hagar felt hopeless, unworthy, unseen, and discouraged about her future. She lacked the ability to trust, she questioned God, she doubted God's existence and love for her, and she probably had little motivation toward survival.

Being a young teenage mother, I felt a range of these emotions. People would tell me that I wasn't a good mother under their breath; others would tell me to my face. For years, I carried around a "fake bag" of lies and believed them to be true. I believed I wasn't good enough, that I was a horrible mom. I doubted my ability to raise a healthy child. I wallowed in self-pity, allowing the blanket of their lies to smother me. These lies became my truth. I felt inferior at school functions. Other moms would turn to me and say, "Oh! You're Rielly's mom. We thought you were her sister. You're a baby yourself." They would then walk over to other moms and whisper to one another, sometimes even giggling amongst themselves.

I quickly learned that I would have to be strong to survive in the den of vipers. I would have to outshine the lies, to be in charge of what I thought to be true despite what others thought of me. I had to learn that, even in my isolation, God saw me. If we allow these feelings to fester, our souls become infected.

Take a moment and read through the list of emotions below. You might be feeling some of these in your current season of life, no matter if it is in parenting, marriage, death, divorce, or some other unraveling.

Don't rush through this list. Give yourself time to pause and consider. Get to the root of your emotions. Ask the hard questions. Ask God to show you why you are experiencing these emotions. Go deep with Him!

Before you consider this list and circle the emotions you're feeling, pray this prayer for illumination.

Lord, I ask that You would highlight the emotion that is trying to keep me entangled. Help me to unravel the pieces in my mind and to get to the root of the issue. Speak to me now, Holy Spirit! Show me that You see me. Help me to understand that You see what I am walking through. Thank you, Jesus.

I am Feeling:

HOPELESS	UNMOTIVATED	SHAMEFUL
UNWORTHY	SELF-PITY	FEARFUL
AN INABILITY TO TRUST	BITTERN	INFERIOR
DOUBTFUL	ANGRY	INSUFFICIENT
APPREHENSIVE	UNWILLING TO FORGIVE	GUILTY
DISCOURAGED	ANXIOUS	DEPENDENT ON OTHERS

Let's look at how Hagar responded to the angel of the Lord as He spoke to her when He found her lying in the desert, next to a spring.

"She gave this name to the Lord who spoke to her: "You are the God who sees me," for she said, "I have now seen the One who sees me.""—Genesis 16:13

When you think life unravels you to the point of no return, when you feel trapped, realize that nothing could be less true. God sees you. He has specific instruction for you and is going to bless you. Because of Hagar's obedience to the Lord's instructions, he blessed her.

Rewrite or think about Romans 8:28 in your own words:

And we know that in all things God works for the good of
those who love him, who have been called according to his purpose.

Judging Hagar

I'll close this chapter with another confession, perhaps worse than my distaste for carnations. I used to judge Hagar. I always saw Hagar as a home-wrecker and a promise-stealer. I always pictured her as the "bad nanny" caricature.

But those assumptions have changed. My eyes have been opened to the truth. When we leave the judging to God alone, we leave space for Him to truly unravel our immature understanding and replace it with kingdom wisdom.

Our lives might look like big messes right now, but God sees us. You don't have to be a pastor or theologian to understand that. No matter how alone you feel, just remember that God protected Hagar. He protects us, too.

Let Us Pray

Lord, I ask You to step into the situations where I feel unseen, where I feel all is lost or beyond repair. Thank You for seeing past my current situation and loving me enough to allow me to walk through the mess. Thank You for the times I am among a crowd yet feel alone. Thank You for those places where I speak and no one responds. Those times I give my heart and am rejected. Thank You for seeing me.

God, help me to feel as if Your arms are wrapped around me, holding me secure. Help me to understand that You see everything taking place. Lord, I declare my trust in You. I declare that You see me, You see these circumstances, and You're the God who promises to take this mess and use it for Your good. It might not look how I envisioned it, so help me through this. Help me to hold fast to Romans 8:28. Help me to have the ability to see past my circumstances, like Hagar did, with Your grace. Let it be done, Lord, in Your Name! Amen.

Chapter 4

HIS WAYS OF BUILDING ARE NOT OUR WAYS

God's way of unraveling and building us is probably different than we would plan. But He never lets us down.

After my husband and our oldest daughter went to look at potential colleges, I received a call from him. He shared that she had figured out what she was going to do with her life.

He said, "Don't laugh. It's not a joke. She is serious and excited!"

"Well, why don't you give me a heads up so I have a moment to process it all and have helpful feedback?"

Cort giggled and said, "No, this is more fun. And I don't want to steal her thunder. I'd rather see your reaction in person. It will be priceless!"

The scenarios played out in my mind. I convinced myself that she had chosen to go to the University of Alabama, betraying the Vols orange. I walked myself through a thousand possibilities that, of course, were all negative. I felt myself spinning out, so I got in the shower. The shower is my prayer closet, my safe space. I started practicing my response to whatever my daughter would tell me. I forced out my best, "Oh, that sounds great!" and could feel how phony it felt. Eventually, my practice time ended when they walked through the front door.

My daughter greeted me with a hug, beaming with pride. Thankfully, she couldn't contain her secret any longer than I could bear not knowing, and she declared that she wanted to major in concrete.

"What did you say? Like, you want to drive a dump truck?"

All my hours of shower-practice failed me in the delivery of this news. The pep drained from my face. I stared at Cort, eyes wide. He knew this look translated to, "Just wait until we are alone in our room, mister. I'll give you a piece of my mind!"

But in that moment, I had to refocus on my baby girl. She looked and acted like Malibu Barbie, and she just decided that she wanted to be Construction Barbie. The child didn't even know the difference between a flat-head and a Phillips screwdriver. Her idea of manual labor is more like dancing and singing.

She stuck to her resolution. She graduated from high school and we dropped her off at her college dorm. Her freshman year came and went, and she nailed it!

During, her sophomore year, she was one of the few girls selected to attend a national concrete conference in Las Vegas. That same year, she called to announce that she landed an amazing internship in North Carolina. Her proud daddy ordered her pink construction boots.

Her career choice, as shocking as it first was to me, was going really well.

But at the beginning of her junior year, she discovered that she would need surgery on her foot. With only three semesters left before graduation, her world began to unravel. Little did we know that this would cause unraveling for our entire family. This season was unbelievably difficult, both as a family and as individuals. God knew these circumstances would impact each of us differently. Of course, Rielly's walk was the hardest because it was her unraveling. But as her parents, we desperately wanted to fix everything. And we couldn't.

The biggest lesson I learned during this season was to love people where they are, not where you want them to be. I felt like a fish out of water, flopping around in my feeble attempts to make everything better for my beloved daughter. I begged God to let me carry her pain. But He simply reminded me to be still, to know that He is God, to entrust her to Him, and to love her right where she was in that moment.

Walking with Someone Who is Unraveling

Watching loved ones walk through trials and "sandpaper seasons" is so hard. You feel powerless to help them. You bargain with God. You try to give your loved one the insight or tools to make it easier. In reality, no amount of worrying, enabling, or telling someone what to do is what God is asking us to do.

Take Job's wife, for example. The Bible says that Job was fearless and upright. He feared God and shunned evil. He was wealthy. Job's wife had a front row seat to his leadership. Then one day, angels presented themselves before God to worship Him, and Satan showed up. He wanted to destroy someone to the point where they would not worship God and instead curse Him. Satan was ready to steal, kill, and destroy Job and his family based on their upright behavior.

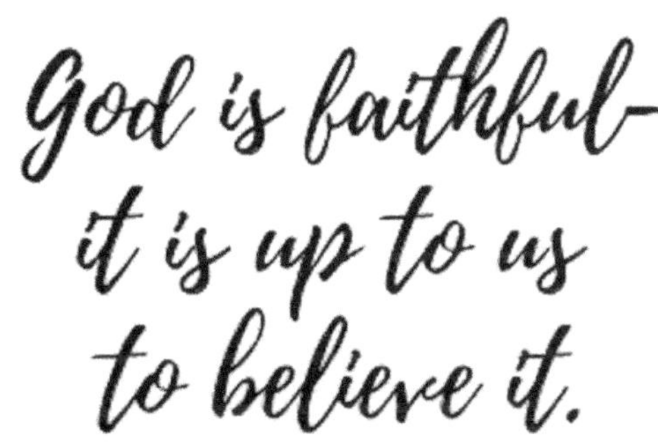

But Satan wasn't the one who chose Job for this trial and temptation. God chose Job. God knew that Job's faith in Him was strong. And God knew that He would be with Job, helping him to endure the suffering. God is the God of the good and the bad. He is in it with us, no matter what. What would be required of Job, then, is unshakable trust in the One who never leaves, even when everything and everyone else does. God is faithful—it is up to us to believe it.

Job was thrust in the middle of deep suffering and pain. His wife, loving him and wanting the suffering to end, encouraged Job to just curse God. But he refused to curse Him.

Sure, it is easy to keep the faith and believe when we are in a season of blessing. But when we are walking in a season of disappointment, we have to say, "God, I don't understand, but You are God." That is hard! So let's look to Job.

Job stood strong with God amidst unimaginable trial. In the end, he defeated Satan, and God was proven victorious, as He always is. Sometimes, God allows suffering to take place in our lives like He did in the life of Job, and even in the life and death of His only Son, Jesus. Our prayer can remain both honest and surrendered. We can say with Job, "God, remove this suffering from my life! But You are God, and You alone."

Are you walking with someone through a season of unraveling? Learn from Job's wife. As much as you want to fix it, it's more fruitful to encourage your loved one through the season instead of trying to "play God" and solve the problem yourself.

Are you walking through your own season of unraveling? Learn from Job's unshakable faith that God is good, even in the midst of horror.

Who do you relate to most in this moment?

Job—Walking through the hopeless, unbelievable, and unexpected circumstances that arrive at your doorstep.

Job's wife—Observing a friend or loved one walk through devastating hardship. You question God and give bad advice, and you might be derailing what God is trying to teach them.

What can we learn from Job's wife about what *not* to do?

What can we learn from Job on what to do?

When we observe a loved one going through a hard time, especially if it is our parents, our children, or our husband, we want to step in and rescue them. In some circumstances, doing this causes us to derail what God is trying to teach them. Honestly, we can derail what He is trying to teach us, too.

> *"Be still, and know that I am God; I will be exalted among the nations,*
> *I will be exalted in the earth." —Psalm 46:10*

Rewrite Psalm 46:10 and apply it to the situation you've been reflecting upon in this chapter.

Many times, we want to offer advice instead of just being present. In the season of Rielly's unraveling, God started to teach me Romans 12:15 in a new way. At first, I hated this verse. I have never been one for pity parties. I am more of a put-on-your-big-girl-pants-and-deal-with-it type of woman. But God commands that we cry and shout with people.

Take a look at the verse below and apply it to your circumstances and the trials of your loved ones. Allow yourself to settle in and trust God as we wait expectantly on Him.

Rejoice with those who rejoice; mourn with those who mourn. —Romans 12:15

Pause and reflect on who you need to rejoice with and who you need to cry with. Fill in the gaps below with one person in your life who is rejoicing, and one who is mourning:

Rejoice with ____.

Mourn with ____.

It's Better to Be Authentic

I hate crying in public. I try to cry in the shower, where people will not see me. So once I understood this practice of shouting and mourning with others, our water bill increased. But God allowed me to learn from Job's wife. The name-it-and-claim-it mentality that is rampant in Christian circles is really an attempted manipulation of God. Blessing God only when things are going well, and cursing Him when trials come, make my life about *me*, not about *God*.

I don't want to be a stumbling block for someone else. I don't want to offer advice when I really don't know what to do. And I don't have to. It's not what God asks of me. Instead, I can rest in Him and love the person as they are through their sufferings. In the end, I must understand that if I derail their unraveling, I delay their freedom.

Let Us Pray

Lord, help me to get out of the way! Help me to be slow to speak and quick to listen. Help me to learn to love ______________________________ exactly where they are. Help me be content in the waiting. Help me to trust in You, not leaning on my own understanding. Help me keep You at the center of my focus so I can rejoice and mourn with others. I need Your strength more than ever, God, because left to my own ways, I am keen to react and behave like Job's wife. Help me to learn from her mistakes. I want to allow Your glory to be seen in me in the midst of unraveling. Let it be. Amen!

Chapter 5

HERE'S THE THING ABOUT YOUR PAST

We can let our pasts shape and control us to the point of disobedience.

We all make bad choices. We struggle through and even regret things about our past. In life, we don't get re-dos, and we can't dwell in regret. You are not your mistakes, your past decisions, or even your regrets. Your fears and shame do not define you. Your mistakes *unravel* you. However, right now, you can use those life lessons as a spring board into the future. Learn from your past. If we can reframe our past mistakes as lessons, not losses, we can gain wisdom to help us, shape us, and prepare us to make better choices for ourselves and for future generations. So we don't lose, we learn.

Our poor daughters have two strikes against them, since Cort and I are both firstborn children. Both of us have a stubborn side. We tend to think that doing it *my* way is the best way. I have justified poor behavior in my life because of this and I have used excuses as a crutch.

Circle any of the excuses below that you have employed when you're asked to obey but really just want to do it your own way. Or, write your go-to excuse in the blank space.

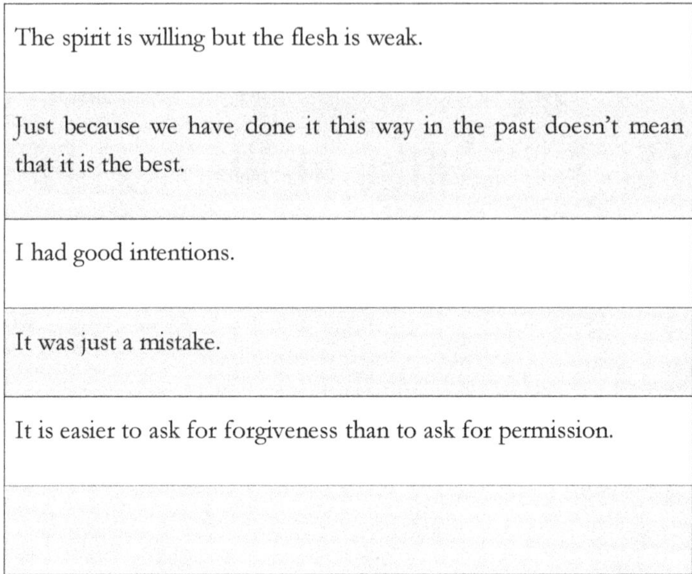

The spirit is willing but the flesh is weak.
Just because we have done it this way in the past doesn't mean that it is the best.
I had good intentions.
It was just a mistake.
It is easier to ask for forgiveness than to ask for permission.

The choice is ours. We can stay stalled in our excuses, or we can come to grips with the fact that the only way forward is to stop looking back. Maybe if we make peace with our mistakes, stop making excuses, and start asking for forgiveness, we can learn what God is truly trying to reveal to us.

Sometimes, when we focus on the past, it makes us long for the former things instead of longing for the new. The former places are normally familiar comforts. While history is something we should always embrace, we should never dwell on or use our past as a crutch.

No Looking Back

Think about Lot's wife in Genesis 12, 13, and 19. Lot and his wife joined Abraham and Sarah when God told them to leave their country. God revealed to them that He was going to make Abraham the father of many nations. During their journey, a famine came to the land. Lot and his wife owned numerous sheep and cattle. Because the healthy land was small, Lot's shepherds and Abraham's shepherds began to fight over it. Abraham didn't want fighting in their family, so he said, "Look, there is plenty of land around here. Pick what direction you want, Lot, and I will go the opposite way."

So Lot and his wife left his Uncle Abraham. They eventually ended up in Sodom and Gomorrah.

God heard the cries of that city and how horribly wicked it was, so He decide to check it out. Abraham was so upset over the situation that he confronted God. Abraham asked God if He was planning on destroying good people with bad people. Abraham knew that Lot and his family were there. So he asked God to spare the city. God agreed and sent an angel to warn Lot that He was going to destroy the city because of all the sin and immorality. The men of Sodom and Gomorrah boxed the angels in and begged Lot to throw them out. The men of the town grew angry with Lot. Lot was yanked back inside the house by the angles. The angels told Lot and his wife that God was going to destroy the city.

At the break of day, the angels pushed Lot and his wife to get going before it was too late. Finally, after numerous warnings, the angels grabbed their arms and dragged them to safety. They instructed the family to refrain from looking back at the city and to run for their lives.

It's hard to let go of what is comfortable and move into a new season. After all, we know *this* place; we have no clue of how things will be in the new season.

Despite the specific instructions and several warnings, Lot's wife just couldn't let it go. Her disobedience cost her dearly. When Lot's wife looked back to watch the city burn, she was immediately turned to a pile of salt. The Bible doesn't say *why* she disobeyed. We can only assume she longed for the former. She didn't want to risk the uncertainty of change.

The message of obedience vs. disobedience is important to all of us who claim to be children of God. While Jesus is our Friend, we can't forget who He is or downplay His position, His authority, or what He did for us on the cross. Sure, I want to be my kids' friend. I want to be in relationship with them. But this desire doesn't circumvent my position in their lives as an authority figure. When we are a child of God, we are in relationship with Him, and we understand what He expects of us.

"If you love me, you will obey what I command." –John 14:15

Rewrite that verse in your own words. How does our obedience show God our love for Him?

Refusing to Be Transformed

In 1 Samuel, we catch another glimpse of this kind of disobedience born from fear. King Saul knew better than to disobey God. But Saul took a ride on the crazy-train and allowed his ego and self-centeredness to inform his thoughts and actions. King Saul knew that, before Israel's army could set off to war, they had to do several things to prepare, both physically and spiritually. Preparing spiritually wasn't a suggestion from God. It was an order. King Saul was to lead the people to seek God for insight and direction in the war. They were to offer a sacrifice and to ask God for His wisdom and guidance. To go into war without God had only lead to failure in the past.

Ultimately, God wasn't looking for a ritual sacrifice from Israel, Saul, or Lot's wife. He doesn't ask that of us, either. God is looking for obedience wrapped up in devotion.

King Saul did offer the sacrifice, but he merely went through the motions. His heart was not positioned toward obedience and devotion. Hence

Samuel, the prophet, said to him, "To obey is better than sacrifice" (1 Samuel 15:22).

When we get into the ritual practices of our worship but lose the devotion and obedience, we lose our rightly-ordered attitude toward God. Too often, we go through the motions like Saul did. Saul wanted to be popular in the eyes of the people instead of being faithful in the eyes of the Lord. He allowed fear of the what-if's to launch him into trying to fix it on his own. Sound familiar? To God, obedience to His Word is more important than worship rituals.

> *"And Saul said unto Samuel, "I have sinned: for I have broken the commandments of the Lord, and thy words: because I feared the people, and obeyed their voice."" —1 Samuel 15:24 (NKJV)*

What excuse did Saul give to Samuel for his disobedience?

It was *fear*!

Forsaking Fear

Take a moment to confess how you have used "Saul's approach." Where has fear prevented you from moving forward in devotion and obedience? When have you wanted to please others more than God? Saul wasn't interested in being uncomfortable in the waiting. He cared more about his own comforts and keeping everyone else happy than he did about obeying what God asked of Him. Where in your life have you done the same?

Think of a situation in your own life in which you were being unraveled by God, but you cared more about pleasing yourself or others, leading you to disobey God. How did that play out in your life? Reflect on this time in your life.

Read 1 Samuel 15:25-29 to see what God did to Saul for his disobedience.

Saul did repent, yet God knew that honestly, his heart wasn't in it. When we long after things that are not of God, we are on the border of actions that will cost us. Saul ultimately lost the kingdom that day. When Lot's wife looked back, she was transformed to a pillar of salt.

Obedience is an important part of allowing God to unravel us. It doesn't always feel great. Sometimes it is hard, and walking away from things we like and people we like is hard. But when God asks us to give up something, He always replaces it with more and better.

There is a time for looking back and a time for looking forward. If you are in a season of being unraveled and God is asking you to let something go, listen. Start by asking yourself questions.

When I start this process, I'm normally crying on the shower floor. I present these questions to God:

"Lord, what is it that I need to let go? Lord, this situation is causing me pain and anxiety. I enjoy doing and being a part of this, but do I need to let it go? God, this show on Netflix sucked me in and I really like it, but now I am dreaming about my husband cheating on me or me robbing a bank. But I don't know how the show ends! Should I let it go?"

When God ask us to give up something, He always replaces it with more and better!

We have to get comfortable with asking God for direction and respecting what He says, whether we like it or not. Obedience is key.

He might be asking us to stop spending so much time with certain people, or to stop watching a problematic show, or to walk away from substances that could possibly spur addiction. Don't hit pause. Agree to God's request before you even think your next thought. Don't look back! Obedience is a call. It is an opportunity to rise to the challenge. Be the overcomer and champion God has called you to be.

Let Us Pray

Lord, help me to not look back when God calls me forward from a place. Help me to not dwell on past sins that threaten to prevent me from moving forward. Help me to deal with any junk and unaddressed issues, then help me to go forward wholeheartedly, with Your grace. Bind me to Your perfect will. I don't want to take one step forward, right, left, or backward without Your protection and guidance. Help me to long for the things of You. Keep me from getting stuck in rituals and routines. Give me a heart to honor You, the King of kings and Lord of lords. Amen.

Part Two

DEVELOPING TRUST THROUGH PRAYER

Have you ever needed something that you didn't have the money to buy, but you knew someone who could give you the "hook up" so you could get that item?

Did you know that, if you're a Christian, you can call on God in those times of need, and He can be your provider? I am not talking about asking for the 2.5 million dollars or the Caribbean cruise. God isn't our cash cow—we cannot make demands of Him. Just because we name it and believe it doesn't mean He will deliver it. I *do* believe that God uses our issues and hardships to teach us to lean in, pray, and ask. He gives us invitations to change our attitudes and our hearts. Ultimately, He will unravel us to the point that, no matter the outcome, we learn to trust Jehovah Jireh, the name that describes God as "provider."

Trusting that God will be our Jehovah Jireh during our unraveling can feel impossible.

Learning to trust an individual, in my experience, doesn't take place in a crowd. Trust takes places in the unseen areas, in the quiet moments. Trusting someone means trusting their character and trusting them to be in your life. Trust is built through one-on-one experiences. I learned to trust God with my pain, my heart, and my feelings during a season of betrayal. I ran away from everyone in my life and retreated with God. I spilled my feelings, I asked the hard questions. Through that experience, I learned that God is slow to anger, that He is good, that He is an active and interested listener. I learned to worship Him alone and to sing alone in the shower. I learned to share my wins and my disappointments with Him. I learned to flee to Him when I fail, and to allow His Word to speak truth to my heart, even when I didn't want to believe it.

When I stepped away from my career in real estate, I spent many nights in my shower-chapel, hiding from my family. I didn't want them to see me shedding desperate tears. It took me months to respond to God's call to shift gears in my career. In fact, it took me five months to build up the courage to even float the idea to my husband. The fact that I felt called to leave a lucrative career to make virtually nothing terrified me. So I battled my own mind, reminding myself of all the times God showed up in the past.

God didn't need the reminder. His character is solid. It was *my* character that needed to be unraveled and reminded of who God was, is, and will forever be. God used my experiences to reveal Himself to me. He was working through me to accomplish His work in and through me. He was teaching me to trust despite what seemed to be impossible, to trust whether I liked this particular season or not.

For years, I made certain that I was in control of my life, my goals, my dreams, and my plans. Heck, I even became the master of fixing and improving everyone around me. I was in the production of my life, and my life was going to be recorded in history books because *I was nailing it*. I wanted to be the expert in all my arenas: PTO mom, business owner, top real estate agent, Jesus lover, hot mom with the rocking body, seasoned mother, and ideal wife. The problem with those goals is that God isn't looking for performance perfection. He is looking for clay, willing to be molded into what He has imagined.

During my nights in the shower, once I finally surrendered to His call, I was in desperate need of a rest and reminder God hadn't changed. The outcome wasn't what I'd hoped, and I needed renewed hope in the One who is always enough. I wanted a fast fix. I wanted God to answer my prayers with the Instant Pot instead of the crockpot.

I developed intimacy with God and became my true self in my conversations with Him. I was more honest than I'd ever been before. And God didn't get tired of me crying; instead, He listened and loved on me. God listened to my broken tune, my pity party. I cried about being alone, having no friends, and feeling like I had no support. Not once did He tell me to suck it up. He received all my emotions, all my pain, and all my raw, real, authentic prayers. The secrets, the shame, and the things I dared not share with anyone else. God was the only One I let in on the secret that I really didn't have it all together.

God had already taught me the importance of prayer during another unraveling experience, but this took my dependence upon Him to a new level. See, when you're real with God and spend time in His presence, there is no room for masks. So put down your mask and receive a fresh release of faith and confidence—not in *your* strength or ability, but in the grace of God.

Eventually, I got over feeling sorry for myself, I stopped crying so much (and praised Him for the disappearance of my puffy under-eyes), and started asking God to teach me what He wanted me to learn.

I came to the Lord day and night. I let Him know that I was frustrated over a lack of response from Him. "Why aren't you answering?" I asked. Then, I would start the cycle over again, thinking that I just needed to pray harder and louder.

Then one morning, He whispered to me, "I don't answer your prayers because of what you do. It isn't because of your "works." It's because of My love. I answer because your heart moves where I need it to be. Don't stop. I am teaching you something great. I am positioning you to receive."

Do you see a theme here, yet again? I came to an end of myself and allowed God to remake me. I set down my armor of perfection and became vulnerable, asking God to speak to me. I learned that prayer isn't the listing of needs and the waiting to be answered; rather, it's a relationship.

I learned to trust that, despite feeling like I was in a pit of darkness with no light to be found, God was teaching me to persevere with patience in my prayer life. He taught me that I can't earn His love. Nothing I do or don't do changes that.

In Part Two, we are going to focus on prayer and how vital it is in our unraveling. We must know how to call on the Name of the Lord and trust that He will answer us, not because of who we are, but because of who He is.

So many of us subscribe to the idea that we get out of something what we put into it. But God isn't like that at all. Some of us refuse to trust a God we can't see, especially when we can't even trust the people around us. Trust is difficult. It requires something of us. It's risky. Yet, taking steps toward trusting God's character is such a breath of fresh air! Look at the thief on the cross beside Christ. He did nothing for Jesus. He simply trusted and asked for mercy. His belief and trust in Jesus earned him a place in heaven. He was in paradise that very day with Jesus! God is so beautiful! When we bow down before Him and open our hearts to that type of confidence in Him, we begin to trust in this radical way.

Let Us Pray

Lord, I owe all to You. Jesus, in those areas where I want to second-guess myself and You, please help me to declare that Your character is great and that You are trustworthy. Remind me of Your truth. When I fail to realize that You shaped the wind in Your hands and dreamed up the plankton in the ocean, remind me. Remind me that You are truly great. Remind me that I can come to You, just as I am, and that You will accept me. Unleash my mouth to speak to You about the big stuff and little stuff in my life. Carve out times and places for us to meet. Thank you for Your mercy and Your patience! Amen.

Chapter 6

NOT A CASH-IN-ON-YOUR-CONNECTION KIND OF PRAYER

Part of learning to trust through prayer is understanding that God isn't our Cash Connection. While we ask God to enlarge our territory, just like Jabez did, we should ultimately want what God wants. His will is what is best for us and He is faithful no matter what.

We first learn of the man named Jabez in the First Book of Chronicles. There isn't much written about Jabez, who he was, or what he accomplished. His name shows up in a long list of names. Scripture mentions what his name means and the prayer he prayed. That's about it.

But we can learn a lot from the prayer of Jabez. Jabez was learning to trust God. He was interested in a spiritual exchange. While his name meant "pain," Jabez exchanged what others said about him for who God said he was. Jabez's request of God shows us what it looks like to trust God's character. Jabez probably felt like he was drowning in words of negativity. He desperately wanted to be truly alive, and he found out that he couldn't make it on his own.

So he went to God in prayer and asked Him to breathe into him. Jabez lifted his head when he uttered his request. He was trying to hold fast to the promises of God. He finally allowed the Lord to carry him through his struggles. Jabez kept moving toward the heart of God. He lifted his head to the Maker of heaven and earth.

*"Jabez cried out to the God of Israel, "Oh, that you would bless
me and enlarge my territory! Let your hand be with me, and keep
me from harm so that I will be free from pain.""* –*1 Chronicles 4:10*

You know what? God granted his request.

Using 1 Chronicles 4:10 as a guide, rewrite the prayer of Jabez in your own words.

Jabez was blessed against all odds. In fact, his mom gave him a name that basically means "causing great pain."

If you're a mom, you know well the joy of telling and re-telling your child the story of their birth on their birthdays. It's our right of passage. It is a badge of honor. We love to talk about how many pushes, stitches, and the hours of pain we endured to give them life. We even share about the pains following birth. We recount how we thought we would die when the nurse told us that we had to go to the bathroom before leaving the hospital. When faced with that choice, I thought to myself, "Well, this place can't be too bad. They bring me three meals a day! Of course they aren't the best meals, but I don't have to cook and clean up." So, I let my nurse know that I might just stay in the hospital for good instead of having to go to the bathroom. Going to the bathroom seemed completely unreasonable after spending the last six hours pushing a watermelon through a golf-ball-sized hole.

When I think of Jabez's mom assigning him that name, I have to imagine that she went through something similar during birth. No doubt about it, with the selection of his name, Jabez's mom reminded her child of what she went through.

I am sure Jabez felt unwanted, maybe even guilty for the unwanted pain he caused his mom. Yet Scripture tells us that Jabez was more honorable than his brothers, and so he cried out for God.

When I read the prayer of Jabez, I can't help but reflect on a man who might have been unraveled by life. Even his name unfairly labeled him. But he didn't let that stop him. God saw him. God never left his side. And when Jabez realized that who other people thought he was wasn't who God created him to be, he allowed the unraveling experience to set a fire in his heart. That burning feeling inside compelled him to cry out, believing that God would provide a new destiny. He desired to be extraordinary despite his ordinariness.

Get to Working, Get to Praying

When God unravels us, it can feel unfair. But if we allow Him, God will bring new desires into our hearts. Some of those desires will be greater than what we could ever imagine or accomplish on our own. No amount of talent, grit, or skill can make those kinds of dreams a reality. God is patient. He is waiting for us to cry out with passion and boldness. Oh, that *You* would bless me, indeed.

In his book, *Prayer of Jabez*, Bruce Wilkinson states, "To bless in the biblical sense means to ask for God's blessing, we're not asking for more of what we could get ourselves. We're crying out for the wonderful, unlimited goodness that only God has the power to know about or give to us."[1] Wilkinson reminds us that Jabez ultimately left it up to God.

Jabez's radical trust in God's goodness has nothing in common with what the popular church culture preaches today, encouraging us to ask God for a Cadillac, a six-figure income, or other material items. God is not our vending machine. If you want to drive a Bentley, if you want to make six-figures, get to work! You can obtain those through your own skill and hustle.

If you want to walk in your purpose and accomplish what God has put you on this earth to do, get to praying!

In the space below, describe a time in life when you were unraveled to the point of pain.

Many of us feel like we are running on empty. Yes, we have come far through our painful unraveling, but we're nowhere close to our comeback. Let's exchange our fears for His truth. Our pain for His purpose. Let's build a firm foundation. Freedom and trust make their mark, and God invades more territory in our heart. We can't carry the weight of our past. When we allow God to be our hope, we can see how our pain can be used for God's purpose. Jabez was a pain survivor. He found redemption on his knees.

Explain how some pain you've experienced has been or could be put to purpose for God's kingdom?

Keep Knocking

For years, I believed that I lacked faith or trust in God. I was praying the same prayers over and over again only to discover that pain, division, and heartache were endlessly knocking on my door. Thankfully, His love came crashing into my prayer time. He pulled me out of the fire of Satan and his lies. It was a process, a true battle. I would declare God's truth one day, and then the next day, fear seeped into every cell.

*"Ask and it will be given to you; seek and you will find; knock
and the door will be opened to you. For everyone who ask receives; the one who
seeks finds; and to the one who knock, the door will be opened." —Matthew 7:7-8*

What does the verse above say about what God does when we ask, seek, and knock? Write the verse below.

When we are willing to keep pounding on Heaven's door—even during times of unanswered prayers, silence, disappointment, and pain—we will find Him. He will open His door.

Perhaps we need to take a play out of Jabez's playbook. We need to decide and declare that our lives are not intended to be riddled with pain. Our circumstances do not define us anymore. We will keep asking, seeking, and knocking. Because just like Jabez, our hearts and honest prayers are honorable in God's eyes.

Ask God for a new dose of faith in His ability to do the impossible, to bring purpose from pain. Write your prayer below and date it.

*Ask God for a
new dose of faith
in His ability to do
the impossible.*

Courage

God doesn't judge a man on his outside appearance. God looks at the heart. God knows exactly what He has placed in you. He is refining you for greatness, even now. Never doubt that God will bring good from the trials in your life. God doesn't allow bad things to happen just so we'll be better people. But when bad things inevitably happen, God uses them for our good. He allows these situations to prepare us for the future. He allows them to shape us for His plans and His purpose.

Don't allow the trials and unraveling be for naught. Instead, allow God to ignite a fresh sense of bravery in your heart for the endeavors He has planned for you. Allow Him to increase your influence in your arenas of life.

We live this out by paying attention to those with whom we interact on a daily basis, by serving them, by letting them know we see them. Our actions influence others in our lives. Our actions open doors and extend invitations. If people don't accept, don't fret. You did the work of planting the seed. Our job isn't to convince—that work belongs to the Holy Spirit. Our job is to be courageous and invite. Allow Him to move through you so that His Name might be known and praised.

When life unravels us, we can decide to stay put and settle, or push through and pray boldly. When we unravel, when life gets difficult, will we lift up God's Name and cry out to Him? Will we continue to ask, seek, knock, and trust? Or will we shutter in fear and accept our unraveling as a failure?

Think of the times when you lose your car in the parking lot. You come out of the grocery store, fail to remember where you parked, and press the panic button. The prayer of Jabez is our spiritual panic button. We send up a loud prayer that doesn't go unnoticed in the spiritual realm. We declare our trust in God despite our pain. We exchange our list of desires for the reality of God's ways.

When we trust God in prayer and allow Him to work through us so that His plans can be realized in our lives, we are cashing in on Who our God is, not what He can do for us.

Let Us Pray

Lord, so often I am overwhelmed by all my needs, wants, timelines, and the labels others give me. I lose sight of who You are. You are the Creator of heaven and earth. You work all things together for my good. You use my imperfections and the things that were meant to harm me for Your good and glory. God, You see me in my past and You know exactly where You are taking me now. Help me to step out in faith and trust You. Help me trust that Your ways are higher than mine. Help me let Your truth refine me. Give me a hunger and desire for Your Word. I love you, Lord! Expand my territory and protect me; nevertheless, Your will be done, Lord! Amen.

Chapter 7

THE EXCHANGE

No matter what our lives look like right now, we must trust that God has a plan. He has a carefully-plotted plan for the *unravel* season, the *revealing* season, and the *launching* season. With each season, we must exchange our finite perspective for God's infinite perspective.

This is what we do when we pray The Lord's Prayer. We use this model, given to us by Jesus Himself, to hand Him our earthly understanding in exchange for His heavenly vantage point.

The Songwriter and the Vocalist

When we pray, "Thy will be done," we declare to the Lord, to Satan, to the demons, and to the angels that the all-powerful God is in charge of our lives. In this request, we beg the Lord for His perspective on what we are facing this very day. Don't treat The Lord's Prayer with meaningless repetition. Instead, use it as a guide. God wants you to add your own flair and personality to this exchange. Add details about your struggles and joys, the good and the bad. God provided the formula, we make it our own. In prayer, we do co-create with God. He sets the stage and invites us into His production and preform alongside Him.

Picture two musical artists, the vocalist and the songwriter. Walking into the studio, the vocalist is handed a musical composition and is commissioned to create a melody from the structure the songwriter has created. She adds the musical inflections and tones to bring life to the songwriter's vision. God is the great Songwriter, we are his vocalists. God gave us the melody for prayer. We create the tone, pitch, and intensity while adding in the vibrato and crescendos with our life's prayer. God desires our praise in this way. He covers our mistakes, understands our needs, offers dependency, and provides direction and protection. All of you plus all of Him creates the life He has designed and destined for you.

> All of you plus all of Him creates the life He has designed and destined for you.

On Rodents and Rescue

Prayer isn't an attempt to get God to see or do it our way. It isn't meant to be a tool used to force God to agree with us (as if we could do that). Prayer is ultimately a reminder to *us* of God's holiness and righteousness. Prayer is about unraveling *our* desires, wants, ways, and purposes to bring God glory. Prayer is our weapon against the world, the devil, and our faulty vision.

If any insects or rodents ever show up in my house, I always immediately call my daddy. Our family owned an extermination business, so I grew up watching my dad fight all kinds of creepy, crawling things. I chose to play my part in the family business in the marketing department, far far away from the "action."

A few years ago, I was home alone one afternoon when one such uninvited house guest arrived. I caught a glimpse of the furry gray body scurrying across my living room floor. Now, I *wanted* to stay calm. I'm a grown woman, I've handled worse. I knew I *should* stay calm. Instead, I fell into a

Tennessee two-step, added a leap, turned to square-dancing moves, and jumped on the couch screaming, "Invader! We are under attack!"

Praise You, Jesus, that I was home alone without witnesses.

But I *was* home alone, which made matters trickier in my mind. No one could hear my cries for help. While most people would have taken a deep breath, left the house, and purchased mouse traps, I wanted to wage a full-fledged war against the mouse (whom I had now named Ralph, naturally).

I knew that, in order to be victorious in the way I craved, I need the right kind of backup. So I called my daddy.

"Daddy, I have a mouse, and I need it gone."

My good dad, as always, came to my rescue immediately. Victory was ours! Ralph was eradicated and I could finally return to living in peace.

In times of desperation in our lives, we usually turn to our heavenly Father for prayer and instruction. When we're frightened or unsure, we cry out to Him. The Lord's Prayer helps us do this. It is a model for us. It helps us come to God, locking arms with Him against our fiercest enemies. When we take up The Lord's Prayer and work in conjunction with God, we are never home alone. We work together for His victory and His glory.

Competing Perspectives

In John 11, we read about Jesus' close friends, Mary, Martha, and Lazarus. These siblings loved Jesus. They were his "framily" (friends who are more like family). In this account, Lazarus was sick. His health was declining rapidly, so his sisters sent word to Jesus. They didn't just want Him to be made aware of Lazarus' condition, they wanted Jesus to *do* something about it.

When Jesus heard the news, He responded by saying, "This sickness will not end in death. No, it is for God's glory so that God's son may be glorified through it."

Then, instead of leaving immediately, He stayed two more days before going to His friends.

When Jesus finally arrived, Lazarus was dead had been in the tomb for four days. When Martha saw Jesus, she was angry and confused. *"Why didn't you come?! We told you He was sick!"*

Martha and Jesus possessed two very different perspectives on Lazarus' condition. Jesus told the disciples that Lazarus was only sleeping. But to everyone present, Lazarus was clearly dead. But God views death differently than we do. Jesus raised Lazarus from the dead, and Martha eventually got to exchange her perspective on death for Jesus's perspective.

Coming to the end of our perspective and coming to embrace God's vision is what unraveling is all about. It's hard to exchange our truth for God's truth. When we use The Lord's Prayer as a model and guide, that is exactly what we do. We allow God to unravel our prayer life.

When we live in resolve to be passionate about God and His ways, our perspective shifts, even if we don't fully understand or comprehend what He's doing. When we pray, we give God full access to facilitate our lives in a way that will bring glory and honor to Him alone.

Today, take time to reflect on how you can incorporate God's model of prayer into your life. It might challenge you; but it will also flood you with peace.

What was Martha's perspective on her brother's death? How did that compare to what Jesus knew? How did Martha's demeanor and life change after she exchanged her perspective for Jesus' perspective?

We have a choice when life begins to unravel us. We can either look at the problem, or we can look at the promises.

God's Word tells us that every gift comes from the Father above. I challenge you to change your perspective. Begin to focus your prayer on the goodness of Christ, looking for the promise in the midst of a problem.

Let Us Pray

Father, You are Holy! I praise Your Name! Lord, today I ask that Your kingdom come, and the Your will be done in me. Today, I ask that You give me a Scripture passage that will be my bread. Help me to stand strong and eat of Your Word and truth.

God, forgive me for my lack of faith. Help me search my heart for anything that I need to confess to You today. Help me to love and forgive those who have hurt me. Surround me and protect me from falling into the traps the enemy sets for me. You're a good and gracious God! Thank you. Amen.

Chapter 8

SMACK DAB IN THE MIDDLE

When the storms of life rage, we are tempted to panic. Sometimes, we know exactly what we should do, the procedures we should follow. And yet, in our fear, we do the opposite. We flee in the opposite direction, whether physically or emotionally.

Jonah was a man trained in faith. He was a known prophet to his beloved people, the Israelites. These people happened to be God's chosen people, and God fiercely defended them against ungodly nations.

All was going well for Jonah and the other prophets in this position, until Jonah was called away by God to go to Nineveh. The other prophets were told to stay.

Here's the thing about the people of Ninevah: they brutally tortured and murdered Jonah's friends and family. They were a great enemy of the Israelites. Now, God asked Jonah to go to their land, to show them mercy, and to bring the message of God's love to them. Jonah immediately reacted harshly. He straight up ran away from God. He fled from his calling with perhaps more passion than he ever used when prophesying.

I love the irony in the story of Jonah. When I read through the story, my first response is always, "Dude, Jonah, just go to Nineveh. It's closer. It is where God told you to go, and you can't outrun or hide from God. Jonah, why are you wearing your stupid hat?"

I am so quick to throw these stones. I act as though, if I were in Jonah's shoes, I would smile, bow before God, and say, "As you wish, Master!"

Yeah, right.

The story of Jonah reminds me of my own "Ninevites." There are countless ways I'm running from what God is asking me to do. I, too, react harshly. I, too, flee. I, too, make excuses. "There are valid reasons why this won't work," I tell Him.

These are the moments God uses to remove layers of doubt, fear, greed, anger, and jealousy out of my life.

Who, what, or where, is *your* Nineveh? Are you running away from what God has placed on your heart? Why are you running?

Borrowed Faith

The book you hold in your hands was a part of my own unraveling. In order to write it, I walked away from a lucrative career. I feared that my family would suffer financially. I worried about what other people would think. Over the course of five months, God removed doubt, fear, and feelings of inadequacy from my heart. Once I made the final decision, circumstances within my family began to fall apart. Not exactly the confirmation I hoped for when I made this leap of faith.

During this season, our best friends and my prayer group pushed us to persevere. They encouraged me to go to my own Nineveh. Sometimes, we have to borrow one another's faith when the task at hand seems out of reach. That is one of the many reasons God established a church. When life knocks you down and you can't carry on in your own faith, you can be lifted up by your brothers and sisters. You can borrow their faith.

Fish Bellies and Bathroom Floors

In Jonah's effort to run from God, he set sail to Tarish. Once he boarded, he immediately went below deck and fell asleep (all that running from God's call was exhausting). A storm threatened the ship, and the sailors panicked. They prayed to their gods of wood and iron, who obviously can't do a darn thing. Believing the ship to be cursed, they cast lots to determine who needed to go in order to eliminate the danger. Guess who was chosen? Our boy, Jonah, who was still sleeping peacefully below deck.

> *There's no out-running, out smarting, or out-planning God.*

The sailors dashed to Jonah and woke him. Imagine the panic in their voices. I'm reminded of the moment in *Home Alone* when the mom realizes what she left at home and yells, "Kevin!" At the sound of the sailors commotion, Jonah rose. The sailors questioned him. It hit Jonah, and he finally got the point. There's no out-running, out-smarting, or out-planning God. The sailors threw Jonah overboard, and he wound up in the belly of a fish.

I love the drama and the detail of God in this story, yet I hate my own "belly of the fish" moments. Sometimes it takes a stinky location to bring us to our senses. For me, it's often a bathroom stall. I know, it's disgusting. I'm a bit of a germaphobe, so coming undone in a bathroom stall wrecks me. Does God use the stinky places to shake us out of our stinking thinking so that we can reach the end of ourselves and the fullness of Him? It certainly worked in Jonah's case. Let's look at his prayer while he was in the belly of the fish.

"In my distress I called to the Lord, and he answered me. From deep in the realm of the dead I called for help, and you listened to my cry. You hurled me into the

depths, into the very heart of the seas, and the currents swirled about me; all your waves and breaker swept over me. I said, "I have been banished from your sight; yet I will look again toward your holy temple." The engulfing waters threatened me, the deep surrounded me; seaweed was wrapped around my head. To the roots of the mountains I sank down; the earth beneath barred me in forever.

But you, Lord my God, brought my life up from the pit. When my life was ebbing away, I remembered you, Lord, and my prayer rose to you, to your holy temple. Those who cling to worthless idols turn away from God's love for them. But I, with shouts of grateful praise, will sacrifice to you. What I have vowed I will make good. I will say, "Salvation comes from the Lord."" And the Lord commanded the fish, and it vomited Jonah onto dry land. —Jonah 2:2-9

When we get to the end of trying it our way and realize that our way doesn't work, we have to get real with ourselves and with God. When we feel like God has turned His back on us, we have a choice. We can adopt a victim mentality and go down a slippery path of misery. Or we can look up and cry out to Him. With the latter, we can authentically repent and beg God for His mercy.

Journal your own prayer of repentance. A prayer of acceptance of your current circumstances. A prayer reminding yourself who God is and what He's done.

When I was 16 years old, I realized that my choices had very real consequences. I missed my period. Food went down and quickly came back up.

I raised my hand in the middle of Chemistry class and asked to be dismissed—I needed the toilet. As I made my way to the door, a fellow cheerleader announced to the class, "She's probably pregnant! She's been scarfing down burgers and getting sick for over two weeks now!"

Until that moment, pregnancy hadn't crossed my mind. My panic propelled me to the bathroom stall. As I lost my lunch in my own "belly of the fish", I realized what I had done. I fell to the floor, my sins coming to light. It was one of the lowest moments of my life, much like Jonah's time in the belly of the fish. But I felt God's hand of grace in the midst of my mess. In that bathroom, it was just the two of us. And just like God commanded the whale to spit Jonah on dry land, God gave me a second chance.

He Never Leaves Us

My life changed that day. Nine months later, I met my beautiful Rielly. While my reality looked different from what I always imagined, God whispered a verse to me that served as my hope and my guide.

""For I know the plans I have for you," declares the Lord, "plans to prosper you and not to harm you, plans to give you hope and a future."" –Jeremiah 29:11

God spoke His Word to me that day. He told me that His plans were good, that His plans would prosper me, that He wouldn't let harm come. He promised to bring good from my brokenness. While those around me declared that a teenage pregnant girl had no hope, God promised me the opposite.

Write Jeremiah 29:11 in your own words.

Sometimes God unravels us because of our poor choices. Not because He is a mean God, but quite the opposite. He is a God who gave us free will. Even as we sit in the belly of our fish, or sprawled on the dirty floor of a bathroom stall, we can rest in knowing that God is working on our hearts and bringing forth a mighty plan to prosper us. We just have to hand over the reigns.

Let Us Pray

Lord, You are a God of second chances. Thank You for giving me a chance to change, just like You did for Jonah. You show me grace when I feel afraid. God, when I am scared in the face of change, help me to know that You can take my impossible and make it possible. Remind me that Your plans are good. You are making a way, even now, when I can't see how it all plays out. Lord, even in my distress I can call upon You, and You hear me. In this difficult situation, let me see Your heart. Amen.

Chapter 9

PRAYING GOD'S WORD

When we are growing in a relationship and developing trust, each moment builds on the next. The same is true when developing a prayer life. When I first started praying, my prayers consisted of, "God is great! God is good! Let us thank Him for our food."

In my adolescence, I attended a few Christian conferences with my aunt and grandmother. I grew up Southern Baptist. My aunt and grandmother were Pentecostal. Something about the way those people prayed deeply touched my soul. My little sister and I loved going to Sunday night services, occasional Wednesday services, and any revivals or events hosted by the Pentecostal church. The meeting rooms filled with the melodies of heaven. Something about it felt so unique, so alive.

At this church, the pastor would call on the Lord differently. He spoke to God as if He was his best friend, open and free and honest. He wasn't scared of God. He talked to Him with confidence, trust, and boldness. He would quote Scripture back to God. The first time I heard the pastor do this, I thought to myself, "Brother, why are you telling God all His names and what He has done? Am I the only person in the room who knows God inspired the Bible?! Why is everyone saying who God is and what He has done? God doesn't need all you adults to repeat it to Him. He knows it better than you! It was all His idea!"

Later on in life, I came to understand that these people weren't doing this for God; they were reminding *themselves* of God's nature, His character, and His promises.

There was something about praying Scripture in this way that captivated my ten-year-old mind. As I listened, the truth of God's Word sank into my heart and filled it with a peace I couldn't explain. Something about this church intrigued me. I wanted more of it, even though I had no clue what it was.

We were definitely the minorities in church, but this sister grew up on Bible drills, putting on my armor and memorizing Scripture, so I knew exactly what they were talking about. However, when we learned Bible verses in my church, it was for candy or a jewel in my Awana's crown. That wasn't necessarily a bad thing, there just happened to be a disconnect in my mind. Until my time at the Pentecostal church, no one showed me how I could channel the Scripture I memorized as my weapon against the enemy when life unraveled me.

I loved the freedom and passion that these saints brought forth as they declared the truth, "No weapon formed against me is going to prosper!" (Isaiah 54:17). I was a dancer, so I got down and praised Jesus with them! I shook my finger, sang loud and proud, and bounced to the beat as I declared praises and truth. "What the enemy meant for evil, my Lord God will use for good! My heavenly Father is the Maker of heaven and earth! He is the Alpha and the Omega!"

These were verses I had memorized at a young age, but I never thought to use them in prayer until that seed was planted. I hid them in my heart and memorized them for Sunday school, but the idea of actually praying the Word over specific situations intoxicated me.

Setting Reminders for Ourselves

Over the years, my prayer life has grown from the foundation I received from the various traditions I was exposed to in my childhood. God used life trials and hardships to unravel me. I'm convinced that I would not have clung to Him in the midst of such messes without having learned to pray God's Word directly over my life in specific and profound ways.

Through my work in real estate, I had a front row seat to many people who used prayer as a final effort when they felt their home wasn't going to sell fast enough, or to obtain the price they wanted. When hardship comes, people quickly remember to pray or want you to pray for them.

But prayer should not be something we do solely when life is unraveling us. It shouldn't be a last resort. It should be something we see as an honor and privilege. It is such a privilege for us to be able to open the 66 books of the Bible and to encounter God in those pages. We learn about Him, we see His track record of fidelity, we witness that God is the same yesterday, today, and forever.

In the second chapter of the Book of Deuteronomy, Moses reminded the Israelites who they are; in the fourth chapter, he reminded them of who God is. These words do the same for us today. We should all form our concept of who God is and who we are in Him through the Word. Because when we go through seasons of unraveling, God will use them to do one thing: to invite our hearts to grow in trust. We may not understand His ways, and our unraveling can foster confusion, but when we look to God's Word, we remind ourselves of God's vision and providence.

"My presence will go with you, and I will give you rest." –Exodus 33:14

The Israelites were in the midst of a complete life-upheaval, and God reminded them that He would lead them and go before them.

The books of the prophets tell story after story of Israel's desperation and the Lord's patient reminders of what He had done for them. God planned prosperity for the Israelites, but they looked to the right and to the left. They disobeyed God's laws. They wanted an earthly king like other nations. They forgot the sweetness of God's boundaries and the fact that the King of kings was their ruler. They took God's protection for granted, forsaking Him, but assuming He would always be there for them.

How often do we do the same?

When they fell prey to their enemies or their own desires, they would cry out to God. Of course, He would answer.

UNRAVELED

"My purpose will stand, and I will do all that I please. From the east I summon a bird of prey; from a far off land, a man to fulfill my purpose. What I have said, that I will bring about; what I have planned, that I will do." –Isaiah 46

When our family was in the process of moving from Texas to Tennessee, we were given three weeks to pack up our house, sell or rent the house, find a home in Tennessee to rent, close our law firm, move into the new rental house and get settled, and register our girls for school. To say our lives were in upheaval doesn't come close to accurately illustrating our situation. Yet, even in the stress, doubt, confusion, and hiccups, God moved mountains. It wasn't always pretty, and there were times we felt like everything would crash down around us. But God did it all.

Finally, we hit the road for Tennessee, believing the worst was behind us. Until we reached the Mississippi River bridge on the boarder of Tennessee and our windshield began sliding off the front of our car.

I couldn't even. What in the world was happening?! But Cort looked at us all and said, "We are so blessed! Let's praise Him in the good and in the bad!"

Mentally, I wasn't there yet. I was planing on calling the dealership. But in that moment, Cort loaned me his own confidence in God. I wish I could tell you that things got better from there, but in fact, things got more complicated. There were delays and miscommunications and disappointments. But God used all of these inconveniences to bring us to the church we were destined to join. My first words to my new pastor were, "I hope y'all are strong, because we have some heavy stuff." He laughed and responded, "We are a tough bunch and are used to lifting and moving." I knew that we had arrived home.

God's protection and plan over our lives isn't short-range. He sees it all and knows it all, just like He knew the ups and downs His people would experience. He is never surprised. He is always ready.

When we apply Scripture to our specific life circumstances, we gain an unshakeable confidence in Christ. When we get to the end of ourselves, trying to figure out the how's and why's, and come to the Bible, let's allow the Word to refresh our souls and minds. Then, we will receive an unwavering peace in our hearts.

He is never surprised. He is always ready.

Speak It Out, Speak It Over

If you want to learn how to pray with Scripture, the best place to start is the Psalms.

David was a man after God's own heart (1 Samuel 13:15). He faced trials and hardships and committed grave sins. He lived through many seasons of unraveling in which God shaped him more and more into the man he was created to be.

In Psalm 3, we see that David was on the run from Absalom, his own son who planned to overtake his kingdom. David spent many years hiding out from Saul and hanging out in a cave surrounded by people wanting to kill him. David knew that in the face of fear, threats, or worries, he needed to do but one thing…He needed to pray!

In David's prayer in Psalm 3, we see his deep trust in the Lord. David didn't have confidence in the reports of men, claiming that God would not deliver him. Instead, David declared, "You are my shield around me, O Lord; you bestow glory on me and lift up my head. To the Lord I cry aloud, and he answers me from his holy hill" (Psalm 3:3-4).

If we want David-like faith in the midst of trials, we must allow God to teach us to rely on Him through storms. When God unravels you, go to the Word. Call out and speak His truth over your situation.

I'm sure my kids think I'm crazy when I pray. I am loud and proud. I am confident that my Lord is going to show up! Don't get me wrong, I still get knocked down. But the older I get, the less I stay on the ground and the more I stand in the truth of Who is fighting for me.

Let's spend a moment with the Psalm below. This will help us learn to pray the Word and stand strong when God unravels us, unravels our thinking, and remakes us so that His glory can be shown.

"Answer me when I call to you my righteous God. Give me relief from my distress; have mercy on me and hear my prayer. How long will you people turn my glory into shame? How long will you love delusions and seek false god?

Know that the Lord has set apart his faithful servant for himself; the Lord hears when I call to him. Tremble and do not sin; when you are on your beds, search your hearts and be silent. Offer the sacrifices of the righteous and trust in the Lord. Many, Lord, are asking, "Who will bring us prosperity?"

Let the light of your face shine on us. Fill my heart with joy when their grain and new wine abound. In peace I will lie down and sleep, for you alone, Lord, make me dwell in safety." –Psalm 4:6-8

When you speak the Word aloud and apply it to your own circumstance, you are confirming it to yourself! You are learning to stand and trust God in the midst of life's storms.

Let's try another verse, this time from the New Testament.

"Those who live according to the sinful nature have their minds set on what that nature desire; but those who live in accordance with the Spirit have their minds set on what the Spirit desires." –Romans 8:5

This is how I would pray it over my own life:

> *"Lord, help me to refrain from setting my mind on the things of this world. Help me to not care about the possessions the world says I need. Instead, Lord, help me, Tiffany Bethmann, to live in accordance with the Spirit. Help me to set my mind on the things You say are good. Help me to only desire the things of Your kingdom!"*

Now, journal your own prayer based on Romans 8:5. You can get more specific and name the particular earthly desires you have and pray specifically for a spiritual desire exchange. Maybe you get angry easily and frequently. Plug that into the natural desire part, and then plug self-control into the spiritual desire part. There is no right or wrong here! Just take the step to open up, speak to the Lord, and start praying His Word.

Let Us Pray

Lord, teach me Your ways. Give me a desire to honor and love Your Word. Help me to have a kingdom perspective. Give me a holy exchange in my actions and thoughts. Set me apart from the things of this world. Fill me with Your Spirit and remove the desires of my flesh as I live this day. God, it is easier to operate in what feels normal, yet I desire Your ways! Help me to declare Your truths and speak them over my life! Amen.

Chapter 10

A PRAYER OF PETITION THAT PRODUCES CONFIDENCE

The fascinating story of Hannah is tucked away in the First Book of Samuel. We learn that she "shared" her husband with another woman. We don't have to be the smartest cookie to know that this family had major problems. Can you imagine the issues that family faced? One man, two wives. Add the fact that one wife can have kids and the other is barren. The husband favors one wife, and the other wife is jealous. We know well that, for women in those days, having a baby was everything. Your identity and worth were determined by your ability to bear a child. It made you feel accepted, secure, and significant.

Since Hannah was unable to have a child, her identity was lost. I would venture to say that Hannah might have been the most miserable, depressed, lonely person in the world at that time.

Have you lived through a season in which you are surrounded by people, but feel alone and worthless?

1 Samuel 1:7-11 speaks of Hannah's soul-condition by revealing, "she was in bitterness of soul." She wanted one thing in life. She wanted to have a child. But in reality, she found herself in an open marriage, unable to have a baby, struggling with an eating disorder. To make matters worse, the other wife was making fun of her and mocking her.

Naturally, Hannah found herself at a crossroads in life. When life dished out pain, she was lonely and cast down. She needed to make a change, and she knew she couldn't change her situation—only God could. She had enough of the torture, enough of the worthlessness, enough of the shame, enough of the spinning out of control. She made a decision. She decided to get up, go to God, and pray.

This is the crux of the chapter. When Hannah unraveled and reached the end of her own efforts, she ran to God. Unraveling is coming to the end of ourselves and coming to God.

Unraveling is coming to the end of yourself and coming to God.

Where do you need to come to the end of yourself?

Hannah decided to pray through the pain. 1 Samuel 1:10 states that in her deep anguish, Hannah prayed to the Lord, weeping bitterly. That God would allow pain to unravel us is not a popular idea in today's world. But if we look closer, we see His goodness and mercy. Even though our pain is never God's intent or desire for us, when we do find ourselves unraveling,

God uses that pain to bring us closer to Him. He really does work all things together for those who love Him (Romans 8:28).

Our Worst Unraveling

We all have crazy in our families. We've all weathered out-of-control seasons in our family. In those seasons, we often feel unaccepted, insecure, and insignificant.

My husband and I lived through a monumental unraveling within my family. That night, the night the thread broke lose, is eternally etched in my mind.

The faces, the choices, the betrayal.

This unraveling blindsided us. The betrayal was confrontational and deeply painful. It ushered in major division in our extended family. It fractured my family, my trust, and my heart. You never dream that your dearly beloved family would betray you. When it happens, it's suffocating. I tried to gasp for air, falling into my husband's arms with heaves and sobs. I was in denial, I couldn't believe—I didn't *want* to believe—what happened. We were paralyzed with shock, fear, and anger. But we needed to move.

After about an hour of staring at one another in confusion, we knew exactly what we needed to do. Broken and bitter, we worshipped our Lord and cried out to Him with a zealous prayer. We knew we were hopeless. Our identities had been crushed to the core. Everything we knew to be true was shattered. Our only hope rested in our Savior coming to our rescue.

Which is exactly what the Lord did. He answered us. He allowed an unraveling to take place in our lives so that He could rebuild us.

When you go through a season in which your soul is deeply bitter, your identity is shaken. God uses this to remind us that He isn't our little rock, but our big rock. God allowed that season to teach me that *I am accepted by Christ.* I stood on the truth of the Bible. God showed me that, despite what I was facing and what my circumstances looked like, I was secure in Christ.

He showed me that I was significant in Him. He did this by teaching me to pray through Scripture using my own name. My prayer life went from decent to zealous. I wouldn't be able to now pray with such trust and conviction if God didn't permit and lead me through some of these most difficult trials.

Remember Who You Are

During my worst unraveling, I clung to Scripture. It became my oxygen tank to the point where I wrote dozens of verses on index cards and hung them around my house. I even stuffed them under mattresses. No matter where I was when desperation or sorrow rose within my soul, I could look up, find a Scripture verse, and remind myself of the truth.

Choose a few verses from the list below and pray through them. Write them in your own words. When the Scripture verse includes words like "you" or "us," replace those words with your own name, and realize that God is speaking His Word directly to *you*.

"How great is the love the Father has lavished on us, that we should be called children of God! And that is what we are! The reason the world does not know us is that it did not know him. Dear friends, now we are children of God, and what we will be has not yet been made known. But we know that when Christ appears, we shall be like him, for we shall see him as he is." –1 John 3:1-2

"Consequently, you are no longer foreigners and strangers, but fellow citizens with God's people and also members of his household..." –Ephesians 2:19

"You are the salt of the earth. But if the salt loses its saltiness, how can it be made salty again? It is no longer good for anything, except to be thrown out and trampled underfoot. You are the light of the world. A town built on a hill cannot be hidden." –Matthew 5:13-14

"Therefore, as God's chosen people, holy and dearly loved, clothe yourselves with compassion, kindness, humility, gentleness and patience." –Colossians 3:12

"What, then, shall we say in response to these things? If God is for us, who can be against us? He who did not spare his own Son, but gave him up for us all— how will he not also, along with him, graciously give us all things? Who will bring any charge against those whom God has chosen? It is God who justifies. Who then is the one who condemns? No one. Christ Jesus who died—more than that, who was raised to life—is at the right hand of God and is also interceding for us. Who shall separate us from the love of Christ? Shall trouble or hardship or persecution or famine or nakedness or danger or sword? As it is written: "For your sake we face death all day long; we are considered as sheep to be slaughtered." No, in all these things we are more than conquerors through him who loved us. For I am convinced that neither death nor life, neither angels nor demons, neither the present nor the future, nor any powers, neither height nor depth, nor anything else in all creation, will be able to separate us from the love of God that is in Christ Jesus our Lord." –Romans 8:31-39

"…made us alive with Christ even when we were dead in transgressions— it is by grace you have been saved." –Ephesians 2:5

"Therefore, there is now no condemnation for those who are in Christ Jesus…"
–Romans 8:1

"…being confident of this, that he who began a good work in you will carry it on to completion until the day of Christ Jesus." –Philippians 1:6

"For through him we both have access to the Father by one Spirit." –Ephesians 2:18

"Let us then approach God's throne of grace with confidence, so that we may receive mercy and find grace to help us in our time of need." –Hebrews 4:16

"As God's co-workers we urge you not to receive God's grace in vain."
—2 Corinthians 6:1

"…and in Christ you have been brought to fullness. He is the head over every power and authority."—Colossians 2:10

"For you died, and your life is now hidden with Christ in God."—Colossians 3:3

"In him and through faith in him we may approach God with freedom and confidence."
—Ephesians 3:12

Hannah's Not Drunk

"As she kept on praying to the Lord, Eli observed her mouth. Hannah was praying in her heart, and her lips were moving but her voice was not heard. Eli thought she was drunk."—1 Samuel 1:12-13

Imagine this moment. Can't you just picture it? Eli walked over to Hannah, thinking he was going to have to escort this crazy, drunk lady out of the tabernacle. But Hannah wasn't drunk; she was sending up an SOS to the Lord with zeal, brokenness, and passion. God collected every single tear Hannah cried, yet this time, something was different in Hannah's heart.

Hannah said to God, "Lord, I want this child desperately. Yet the thing I want the most, I desire so that *You* may use this child to show forth Your glory."

What a beautiful picture of being unraveled by God. There is beauty when we come to the end of our wants and comforts and say, "Lord, not my will, but Yours be done!"

As Hannah ended her prayer, she saw Eli approaching her. She realized what he assumed about her state.

She quickly informed Him, "I am not drunk. I am praying and asking God for help."

Eli was probably a little embarrassed that Hannah knew he was judging her, especially since his own sons were priests and also the town drunks themselves. Quickly, Eli said a blessing and asked God to grant Hannah her request.

Immediately, Hannah got up and left the temple, and sorrow left her heart. Now *that* is an altar experience! She left the pain at the altar and exchanged her pain for trust in God. Scripture said that she was sad no more. This indicated a mental shift, a choice. Her head knowledge of who God was settled down into her heart. She no longer stood in shame, but in confidence in God.

Let's pause for a moment. Here we have a depressed lady, with no child, living in a family she despised. The moment Hannah made a choice to get up and leave her surroundings, her normal, her comfort, in order to go to the house of the Lord, she allowed the unraveling to happen. She positioned herself for an exchange.

First, Hannah went. Second, she prayed. Third, she bowed her head and prayed with Eli and he spoke a prophetic word over here. At last, she stood in confidence.

When life unravels us, Hannah's prayer shows us some practical steps for trusting in God.

Write down the names of two friends, maybe a pastor, who you can lean on during your unraveling and who will be willing to pray with you.

Let Us Pray

For this prayer, we're going to write our own.

In the space below, write a zealous prayer from your heart and date it. Don't sugarcoat anything. God can handle your raw and authentic prayer. Whether your prayer is full of tears or full of cuss words, let your heart cry out. Until we can decided to be real and zealous before our Lord, we are just giving Him lip service. God is big enough to take your pain.

When I was walking through a difficult season in my marriage, God probably thought I was a sailor rather than a southern belle. He loved me through my anger and pain. Not once did an angel appear and deliver a swear jar. I know this kind of honest prayer might seem un-Christian, but the heart of Christianity is the truth that God wants our whole hearts. No filters. No curated captions. Just our hearts. We show great confidence in Him when we bear it all. Let's do that now.

Part Three

DEVELOPING A SPIRITUAL PALATE

The old-fashioned mac and cheese from the blue box was the food of my childhood. Passing the joy of blue-box-macaroni to my own children, it became a staple in the Bethmann home.

One night when my girls were little, our family went to dinner at an all-you-can-eat buffet. All my girls wanted was mac and cheese. Rielly, our oldest and the ringleader, approached the tray of noodles and cheese on the buffet line. I could tell by the look on her face that she was not impressed. Looking up at the server, she asked sincerely, "What's wrong with your mac and cheese? It's not supposed to have sprinkles on it…"

The kind server attempted to explain that this mac and cheese was made with a blend of five carefully-selected cheeses. The "sprinkles" were, in fact, toasted bread crumbs on top of the mac and cheese, making it even more special. Rielly accepted her explanation, but she was still suspicious.

At the end of our meal, we had three full bowls of mac and cheese left on our table. The girls were not used to such rich and varied flavor from their mac and cheese.

Years later, when Rielly was a junior in high school and still living on the blue-box mac, she went to dinner with a friend's family and decided to try lobster mac and cheese. She called me on the way home, too eager to share her life changing news to wait until we were face-to-face.

"Mom, did you know they make lobster mac and cheese?! With several different cheeses! And it has the perfect amount of bread crumbs on top to make it crunchy. You have to try it! It was the best mac and cheese I've ever had!"

We just giggled together, me holding that funny, fond memory of the buffet line close to my heart.

Isn't this just like all of us? We get set in our ways. We grow comfortable with what we know and like. We become a little too stubborn to change. We long for the familiar. And we turn up our noses when God tries to serve us something new. We leave His invitation to greatness on the table until it grows cold and is thrown away.

Go for the Lobster

Just like our palates are meant to mature and expand over time so that vegetables are no longer gag-inducing and we actually enjoy fine cheeses, so too should our spiritual palates develop. We develop our spiritual palates by allowing God to take our "spiritual taste buds" up a notch so we can graduate from blue-box mac and cheese to the lobster version. This process involves removing our cravings for junk and replacing them with hunger for the things of God.

One day, I was driving home from what was another awful day at work. I was upset and frustrated. So I finally got real with God. I yelled at Him, at the top of my lungs, "I know You didn't bring me out here to destroy me! You called me to be a mother, a wife, *then* an employee. But I'm dropping my babies off early in the morning and not seeing them until late at night. I feel like I'm not even a part of their lives! This can't be it; this can't be what You have for me! I would rather work nights, scrubbing toilets, than miss one more day with my kids, feeling trapped in a miserable job. So God, move those mountains! Make a way!"

After my outburst/prayer, I walked into my house. While I was sitting in the quiet of my house, eating a sandwich, I heard the Holy Spirit whisper, "Get on the city's Chamber of Commerce website and make a call."

When I opened the webpage and located the number God directed me to, I laughed. It was a medical sales company. Growing up, I always thought it would be cool to be in medical sales. But I never finished my college degree. In my mind, no degree meant no pharmaceuticals or medical sales. It was always a dream and desire, but I didn't see a way.

Out of obedience to the Holy Spirit's direction, I made the call anyway. The Director of Marketing and Sales answered. She said, "Funny you should call! We are looking for a territory rep in your area. We just decided on this yesterday and we will start interviewing tomorrow." She went on to inform me that the job was a remote work-from-home position. I would receive a company car and a flexible schedule, but I would make less than what my current job paid me. My conviction won out over my comfort, and I decided to go for it.

God desires to develop our taste into a new, sophisticated spiritual palate. In order to do this, we have to allow Him to unravel and remake us. We have to be willing to be uncomfortable, to try something new.

In Scripture, Daniel knew what it meant to trust God in a foreign land. At a young age, He didn't conform to the world around him. Instead, he asked God to set him apart. In other words, Daniel asked God to unravel him for His purposes.

I went on that interview and was hired on the spot. Less than two weeks into my new job, that same woman submitted her notice of resignation. I now had to start from ground zero. I had to develop new territories on my own; I had to train myself. All the while, I was confident that I was the gal for the job.

After my first month with the company, they gave me a pay raise that eclipsed what I was making at my previous job. I had flexibility, I saw my babies, and now, God provided in even the smallest of ways.

God wants only our good. When we allow Him to unravel us, He will surprise us, too.

"Now to him who is able to do immeasurably more than all we ask or imagine, according to his power that is at work within us..." –Ephesians 3:20

Let Us Pray

Lord, I am Yours. I am called, chosen, and highly favored. Even in unfamiliar territory, I can put my trust in You. You aren't just a get-me-by God, but You want to blow my mind. Thank You for being my oxygen tank. Thank You for loving me lavishly and for walking beside me as You unravel me.

Chapter 11

NO COMPROMISE

When we're being unraveled, others watch. We can use our unraveling as an opportunity for witness. Think of the early Christians. They endured massive persecution. I am sure they had moments of doubt, confusion, and fear. They likely felt abandoned at times. But God took what Satan meant for evil (the persecution and killing of Christians) and used it for good (the rampant spreading of the Gospel of Christ to many nations). If we follow God hoping for a life filled with unicorns and success, we will be disappointed. The Christian way is ultimately about leading people to Christ, no matter the cost.

When faced with moments like this, we may be tempted to compromise.

Consider the story of the hunter. The coming winter would be brutal. Knowing this, a hunter went into the forest to shoot a bear for its warm coat. He waited and waited. Finally, he saw a bear coming toward him. He raised his gun and took aim.

"Wait!" said the bear. "Why do you want to shoot me?"

"Because I am cold," said the hunter.

"But I am hungry," the bear replied, "so maybe we can reach an agreement."

In the end, the hunter was well enveloped with the bear's fur, and the bear had eaten his dinner.[1]

Just like the hunter, we always lose when we try to compromise with sin. It will consume us in the end.

Put to the Test

Have you ever found yourself in the predicament of the hunter? You had a plan and a purpose, but something derails your determination and you falter.

When we operate in faith and seek to understand the ways of the Lord, we realize that compromise is just a trap. The trap usually presents itself as a quick solution for getting past the problem. However, we learn from Daniel that part of developing a spiritual palate is refusing and refraining from compromise.

If you have fallen victim to compromise, do not fear, because God is still near. Our choices do have consequences, but let's never mistake those consequences as God's absence or departure. He loves us always.

The Book of Daniel illustrates this refusal to compromise. In Daniel 6, there's a new king in the palace. This king, Darius, wanted to give power to more local authorities. He was in major delegating mode. At this time, Daniel was pretty popular and well-known for his wisdom and ability. He probably even landed himself on the cover of *Babylonia Man of the Year* magazine. Despite being a foreigner, Daniel was put in important positions throughout the kingdom. The rumor mill claimed that Darius planned to promote Daniel above everyone else.

Daniel's peers grew jealous and decided they could not allow it. So they devised a plan to trap Daniel. They knew of Daniel's strong resolve to follow God, and they decided to hit him where it hurt by tempting him to compromise on his beliefs.

Can you think of a time in your life when you had a decision to compromise or stand firm?

Choices and Chocolate

Playing at our neighbor's house one afternoon, I reached into my pocket to discover a candy bar. I had forgotten that I put the candy bar in my pocket when my mom and I stopped off at the drugstore. I froze. That small KitKat had been forgotten because I got distracted, and we made it out of the store without paying. My childhood mind raced. I knew that I had to get to my mom right away before the police were sent to my house to arrest me!

I left in the middle of the game we were playing. This was an emergency. I ran into the house yelling, "Mom! Where are you? It is an emergency! Come quick!"

I have always had a flare for the dramatic. As far as I was concerned, in my elementary-school mind, my life was on the line. It was just a mistake, an accident; but nevertheless, I had to make this right. My whole integrity, our family's name, depended on it.

From a young age, my dad and mom instilled in me the importance of honoring my name. I was constantly told that I wasn't just representing myself, but my family and our family-owned and named business. Because I bore my family's name, my choices reflected upon them. This concept looped in my mind as I waited to tell my mom what happened.

Through my panic-filled words and tears, my mom pieced together my confession. Instead of brushing it off, my mom showed me what it meant to avoid compromise.

Mom called the manager of the store and I told him the whole story. I told him I would return the candy and pay for it. The good news is that the police weren't sent to arrest me, and I learned a valuable lesson.

Following Daniel's Lead

Daniel's religion and principles were his foundation. They lit his way. Daniel would never compromise his faith in God. He would betray Darius and face death before he would compromise his faith in God.

What a weird trap they would create. Of course, Darius had an ego issue, wanting the whole kingdom to bow before him and worship him. Nevertheless, he neglected to see that the one person he wanted to put in charge of everything was a loyal follower of God.

Daniel heard the decree of the king, forbidding anyone to worship anyone or anything else. Every morning, Daniel looked out his window toward Jerusalem, where the presence of the Lord dwelled. He didn't go in front of the window to summon an audience, to solicit likes, or to attract the most views. He simply wanted to be as close to the presence of the Lord as possible, despite where he was geographically.

Daniel didn't question whether or not he would stay true and obey God's commandments over the king's demands. He just acted! He worshipped God openly and with abandon. Daniel did not compromise.

Take a moment to really reflect. Where are you compromising in life or in faith right now?

If you choose to continue to compromise like this, how will you cheat yourself and cheat God?

Small compromises lead to bigger compromises. I choose to compromise when I don't correct the clerk when the shirt I'm purchasing rings up cheaper than it should. I choose to compromise when I yell too aggressively at my daughter's soccer game. These things don't seem like shameful compromises, but what I do in the face of these tiny events forms my heart and prepares my response to bigger events. If I want to be strong and steady during life's big moments, I have to practice in the small moments.

How do we practice? As Christians, we must allow God to unravel our thinking. We must ask God to give us a desire for the things of His kingdom. We want our spiritual palates to align with God's kingdom, and compromising isn't part of God's plan. It is a shortcut. It doesn't mean that you're going to miss out on what God has for you if you've already com-promised. It means that you're called and equip-ped to do better next time.

> *If I want to be strong and steady during life's big moments, I have to practice in the small moments.*

Despite our inadequacies, God dreams a beautiful dream for our lives. He shows us what to do and how to avoid negative consequences through the life of one of His faithful, Daniel.

Let's look at how Daniel avoided compromise:

- He did not question God.

- He did not doubt God.

- He did not worry.

- He trusted God.

- He acted in faith by prayer, refusing to compromise.

Revisit the area where you feel you are either compromising or being tempted to compromise. Let's break it down. Ask yourself these questions before coming to a decision.

If I ____,
will I be compromising any of God's commandments?

God says ____;
so why should I doubt Him and believe this compromise is acceptable?

If I do ____,
the consequences could lead to ___________________________________.

God's Word tells me to ____.

Habits and Choices

The way you develop a spiritual palate that finds compromise distasteful is by developing a habit of prayer. That's right, prayer is a habit. Which means prayer is a discipline. Which means prayer is a choice.

*"Evening, morning, and noon I cry out in distress,
and he hears my voice." —Psalm 55:17*

Daniel made it a habit to cry out to God three times a day. He wasn't trying to launch the newest social media movement and flaunt disobedience to the king. No, Daniel was already in the habit of praying to God and worshipping Him, long before the decree was issued.

So Daniel continued to pray as he always did—in his room, close to the window, looking toward the tabernacle. And the king's spies watched, waiting to bring about his demise.

But God had bigger plans. God knew the character of Daniel. He knew the resolve. He knew that Daniel would be faithful, even as his life unraveled to the point of being shattered. So while the spies and peers saw this as a trap, God saw this as an opportunity.

Daniel was tossed into the lions' den, and God's power shut the lions' mouths. King Darius and the entire nation were brought to their knees. Darius declared that Daniel's God was the King of kings and Lord of lords. All of this came about because one man had a hunger for the things of God and allowed God to develop his spiritual palate. Daniel trusted God, despite how horrible things looked.

Let Us Pray

Lord, plant me in Your truth. Help me to avoid compromise in the small things so I will stand firm in the big things. Lord, remind me that You are like an lion standing over its prey, and like a bird protecting its nest. You will defend me. Help me to live out integrity in the unseen places. Give me a glimpse of what that looks like in Your kingdom. I only need to trust You. Lord, make Your convictions my convictions. Change me to be the beautiful creation You see when you look at me. Keep unraveling me. Use me for Your glory. Remind me that where You are, King of kings, all is safe, all is good, all is cared for, all is provided, and all sins are forgiven. Amen.

Chapter 12

ONLY ONE

Cort had planned an anniversary trip to Jamaica. We were both excited for this time away together, a time to relax and reconnect, a time to rest and rejuvenate. Our journey there, however, was not as life-giving.

Our first flight experienced intense turbulence, leaving us both a little nauseous and even more ready to reach our destination. We had to run to make our connecting flight, which didn't help our turning tummies. When we were getting ready to board, we discovered that our seats were middle seats. My 6'5" husband would be so uncomfortable.

I approached the desk to speak with the kind lady. I told her about our initial flight experience, and all about how my husband had planned this romantic week away without our kids. I just wanted to be certain that the next flight would be enjoyable. There were other people around, also pleading their cases for better seats. Suddenly, my zeal overcame me and I mixed up my words. With all vigor and certainty, I told her that the aisle seats were crucial for us because my husband was 7'5". Seven feet, five inches.

Honestly, I didn't even realize my mistake. Her eyes widened, and I knew she understood our predicament. She was very kind and helpful, and although the flight was full, she managed to snag a more comfortable seat for Cort.

I walked back to Cort feeling victorious and proud of what I arranged for him. As I recapped the conversation, I became more animated with glee.

Cort did not respond with the awe and wonder I was expecting. He laughed a little and looked embarrassed. "Are you kidding me, Tiffany? You *do* know that I am *not* seven feet and five inches."

I said, "Yes you are, baby!"

Rolling his eyes and laughing, he said, "Tiffany, you just made me taller than Kareem Abdul-Jabbar. I am only *six* feet and five inches."

The Whisper

There are times in our lives when we make things taller. We put them in places and positions that are not meant for them. We make *ourselves* taller. We allow pride, accomplishments, or titles go to our head. Sometimes we worship those things, making them our gods.

Daniel reminds us that there is only One.

The Book of Daniel introduces us to King Nebuchadnezzar. God showed this king that only one King is great, and He sits on the throne in heaven. Through Daniel, the Lord unraveled King Nebuchadnezzar.

When I first read this account, it made me uncomfortable. I didn't like it. God showed me how much I have in common with ol' King Neb. He showed me how much my spiritual palate needed to change, and in what ways I needed to unravel patterns in my life. At first, I was defensive. "Who, me? I am *so* more like Daniel. Or Shadrach, Meshach, or Abednego. I have faith!"

Take it from me, don't argue with God. Just listen and get down to business. Learning to hear God's voice takes some practice. Just like hitting a home run or running a marathon. You have to put some work into it to get the results you desire.

In 1 Kings 18, God gave Elijah a revelation on hearing His voice. Elijah had been busting his tail, trying to show the people the one true God. He was worn out, so he went away to rest. Here, Elijah poured out his heart to God. He was frustrated because his work seemed fruitless. He was preaching the truth, but the people weren't listening. They destroyed everything that is holy. They murdered the prophets. Elijah informed God that he was the only one left. And now, he was going to be killed.

So God told Elijah to stand outside on the mountain and to watch and listen for Him. First, a mighty wind a ripped through and destroyed the rocks in the mountain. Then, God sent an earthquake and a fire. In all that noise, God wasn't there. Finally, God sent a gentle, quiet whisper. When Elijah heard the whisper, he covered his face, because He knew it was God.

When we learn to read the Bible, we learn to hear the voice of God. When I get ready to stand in front of a crowd to speak, everything in me screams, "No way can you do this!" But then a thought arises in my heart and mind, "When you are weak, I am strong."

When we learn to hear the voice of God through reading His Word, He speaks clear messages to our hearts that confirm the truth. He doesn't go all crazy on us. He knows we are trying to progress from crawling to running. It takes time, practice, and intention. We have to make time to sit with the Lord, to read His Word, and to listen for His whisper. The sooner we allow Him to unravel us in the truth of His Word, the sooner we will be filled up with His truth.

Fair Warning

Daniel 4 gives us evidence of this spiritual progression through the unraveling of Daniel. This chapter illustrates God's desire that we all fall under His Lordship and allow His ways to rule and govern us.

In this chapter, we find King Nebuchadnezzar and God in a contest for who is King of kings. King Nebuchadnezzar, in all his splendor and pride, failed to recognize that God is sovereign and full of splendor.

Let's zone in on Daniel 4:25:

> *"Til you know that the most high rules in the kingdom*
> *of men, and gives it to whomever He wants."*

Up until this time, King Nebuchadnezzar had a front row seat to the awesomeness of God. In chapter 3 of Daniel, we saw how King Nebuchadnezzar, in his rage, tossed the three friends, Shadrach, Meshach, and Abednego, in the fire. King Nebuchadnezzar witnessed a fourth dude in there, and claimed publicly that he looked like the son of gods. At the end of the chapter, King Nebuchadnezzar ordered that anyone who said anything against the God of these three friends be cut into pieces and their houses be turned into piles of rubble. It appeared that he believed.

Later, in chapter 4, we see how God used a dream to unravel the king a bit. The king had no peace. His mind was being tormented with doubt and fear. Even though he trusted and honored Daniel, he didn't immediately turn to him for advice.

God doesn't look for compliant hearts, He looks for conformed hearts.

When Daniel was finally called to the palace, he hesitated to tell King Nebuchadnezzar that he knew what the dream meant. King Nebuchadnezzar's earthly possessions and accolades would be wiped away. Daniel saw that King Nebuchadnezzar would act and eat like an animal. He would, essentially, lose his mind. The message was one of judgment, but also one of condition. Daniel warned the king to avoid thinking of himself as a god. He told him to be humbled and kind instead of focusing on his wealth and achievements.

In verse 28, God revealed that He would not stand for things that tried to take His rightful place, and He dealt with King Nebuchadnezzar quickly. The Scripture says that King Nebuchadnezzar was temporarily compliant to Daniel's warning out of fear. But God doesn't look for compliant hearts, He looks for conformed hearts.

After a year of heeding Daniel's warning, Babylon obtained two of the Seven Wonders of the Ancient World: the hanging gardens and the city walls. So the king was ready to toot his own horn. Nebuchadnezzar allowed pride to enter and consume his heart.

But God, then and now, remained the greatest Wonder of the World.

Have you ever made an unthinkable claim, or claimed credit for something that you did do but forgot Who gave you the initial abilities to do the unthinkable?

God commands us to worship Him alone and to forsake all idols. Most of us don't have golden calves in our backyards. But we do have mini idols that threaten to sit on the throne of our hearts—the throne that belongs to the one God.

Mini Idols

Take some time to sit with this list. Ask God to speak to your heart. Listen for that quiet voice. Be honest with yourself. Admit the people, things, or circumstances that compete with God for the throne of your heart. What on this list gets your attention over God? This is a difficult practice, but I promise it will be worth it. Feel free to circle all that apply.

HUSBAND	HELPING OTHERS	FOOD	HOME
KIDS	BUILDING A BUSINESS	FUN	RESPONSIBILITIES
WORK	APPEARANCE	DATING	WEIGHT
SPORTS	HOW OTHERS SEE US	WHAT WE DON'T HAVE	SALARY
CARS	GOALS	LOVE	MUSIC
TRAVEL	TV	ANOTHER PERSON	OTHER:

At some point in my life, each of these were a distraction for me. So no judgement here! It is hard to come to grips with the fact that I placed these distractions on a pedestal of worship. My energy and my thoughts were consumed by these, not by God. They captivated my time, energy, thoughts, and heart.

Let's ask God to help us to realign our responsibilities. Let's beg Him to reorder our thoughts so that we don't place things or people in His place of worship. What are those unhealthy people, places, or traps of "busy-ness" that take us away from having healthy, God-focused lives? What about the good things in life we are called to, like our children and work? Have those priorities become misaligned? Offer the honest truth to God, even if it stings.

It's easy to dethrone the phone or other superficial things in our lives. It's harder to dethrone the good stuff. I often have to examine my heart in regards to my husband. I'm tempted to put him on the throne beside God. I don't like to admit it, but I do. If I'm at home on a Friday night and have the choice between reading the Bible or watching a movie with Cort, I'm going to choose Cort. This fact gives me an opportunity to realign my priorities.

Everything Daniel prophesied about King Nebuchadnezzar came to pass. He became animal-like and hopeless. He fought against God's unraveling and it made the process more painful. Dethroning the false gods in our lives takes grace and power from God. We must lean into Him during the unraveling. It's part of putting Him on the throne.

Let Us Pray

Lord, help me to dethrone the false gods in my life, especially if those gods are good things. Show me how to make You my top priority while also tending to the people and things you've put in my life. Help me to grow in Your Word and instill in me a love for Your desires. Amen.

Chapter 13

UNDERSTANDING GOD'S GOSPEL MESSAGE

Why is this happening to me? Why has God abandoned me? Is He a good God?

Many of us ask these questions about our world and our lives. It is hard for us to make sense of unraveling, especially if we call Jesus the Lord of our lives. If God loves me, then why is life hard? If God loves me, why is my heart breaking?

We want to believe that God is good, but we wrestle with doubt and fear. We wonder when He is going to kick us to the curb because we've just screwed up too many times.

I get it. I've felt these very real emotions. I love Jesus, but when I turn on the news to see churches attacked, I wrestle with doubt about God's goodness. If God is in control, why doesn't He stop these atrocities? Why doesn't He put an end to child abuse and sex slavery?

If God is truly a good God, why did He allow me to get pregnant as a teenager? Other people slept around much more than I did. And yet He chose to slam me? Or why did He allow my spouse to stop loving me? Why did He allow my family to betray me so deeply? Why did He allow my child to be born with a difficult condition? I believe, Lord, and yet I lose my faith.

For God So Loved the World?

How do you make sense of God's Gospel message in John 3:16-17?

"For God so loved the world that He gave His one and only son, that whosoever believe in him shall not perish but have eternal life. For God did not send His Son into the world to condemn the world but to save the world through him."

How can we trust this Word when everything seems like it's going to hell in a hand basket?

There were months on end I wrestled with these questions. I walked into church, my own mental battles raging, trying to hold fast to faith when all I really wanted to do was harden my heart.

Many of us walk away from our faith because of misunderstanding, stringent rules and regulations, the presence of judgment over grace, gossip and backstabbing, or the hurt we endured growing up in the church. We feel alienated, used, hurt, abused; and still, we cannot find the comfort we seek in the world. There's a reason our hearts can't rest away from Him.

In John's Gospel, the Apostle gives us a basic understanding of who Jesus is and why He came to earth. John tells us that Jesus is eternal, He is the Word that became flesh. He brings life. He takes away the sins of the world. He is the Lamb of God. In John 2, we see Jesus' first miracle of turning water to wine at the wedding at Cana. In this first sign, revealing His glory, Jesus wanted to be discreet. Then the next thing we see Jesus do is cleanse the temple and drive the corruption away. Not so discreet.

I have a rule in my house. Before we leave for a soccer tournament or vacation, the house has to be completely clean. In these two Gospel accounts, John shows us that Jesus wants to cleanse and renew *us*. Believing and understanding the Gospel message brings new life.

John 3:16 is probably one of the most recognized Bible verses by Christians and non-Christians alike. *God loves us*. It's the foundation of everything.

No wonder the devil tries so hard to convince us otherwise.

Never an Inconvenience

Once, when I was in elementary school, I was invited to a friend's birthday party. This party was the talk of the classroom, and we were all excited to go. On the day of the party, I arrived late. My friend's dad was visibly annoyed at our tardiness. Even as a young girl, I could tell that he was irritated with me. For the rest of the party, it was obvious to me that he only put up with me because I was his daughter's friend.

Isn't that how we feel sometimes about God the Father and God the Son? That Jesus had to come to Earth and die on a cross to "make" God the Father love us? We go through life and seasons of unraveling believing that God is barely putting up with us and that He's inconvenienced by our shortcomings. Many of us buy into this lie, so we keep God the Father at a distance, convinced that if He gets too close, His tolerance of us will run dry.

It's sure hard to find peace and joy in God when we don't understand His message of love.

How you perceive the way God sees you will determine how you see Him. How are you thinking about God? How do you view God? Do you see Him as a distant and legalistic God, a puppet master of sorts, without any real interest or investment in you?

Or do you grasp the truth of John 3:16 and see God as a merciful and loving God?

How do we truly change our questioning and doubting into believing?

#Blessed

When we see #blessed accompany a post on social media, it's not typically referring to a cancer diagnosis or divorce. No, it's easy to believe that God loves us when we get the promotion, have a healthy new baby, or buy a new car. But the same is true when we lose a job, when a family member dies, and when our car breaks down unexpectedly.

Let's revisit John 3:16. Really read this passage. Then write it out, personalizing it. See yourself as "the world."

This verse doesn't say: "For God so loved the world He gave His only son so you will never deal with hardship, or pain, or suffering." But we often translate it that way.

If we adopt the mindset that we are only loved by God when joy and goodness are in our life, then we miss the entire point. Our unraveling will be truly unbearable. Christianity calls us to walk by faith, not by sight. We can't judge God's love merely by what we see or don't see. Feel or don't feel. Get or don't get.

He doesn't waver in His love or affection. He so loves us, endlessly and without reserve.

So the next time you walk through an unraveling, don't let your joy fade. When the washing machine quits, when you get a speeding ticket, or when you burn dinner, don't allow yourself to doubt

God's goodness or great love for you. God cares for you enough to step out of heaven and into this fallen earth. He did this so He could have relationship with you, so that you could experience the love of the Father. He doesn't waver in His love or affection. He so loves *us*, endlessly and without reserve.

Let Us Pray

Lord, I don't get You sometimes. I don't understand why You let bad things happen to good people, and good things happen to bad people. Don't let me be blind to Your love, unable to believe when things get difficult. Enter into my heart. Give me fresh revelation of the love You have for me. In Your Name, I take negative thinking captive and claim Your love over my life. Remind me that You, God the Father, don't tolerate me because of Jesus, but that You hold me dear and embrace me because of how much You love me. Give me a deep understanding of Your patience, kindness, and gentleness. Renew my mind with Your truth and love right now!

I seal this prayer in the precious blood of the Lamb, who died and was wounded for me before I ever asked for forgiveness. You called me, loved me, and even hand-picked me to be Yours forever and ever. Amen.

Chapter 14

I'LL TAKE SECONDS, OR THIRDS

The love of the Father can seem so complex. Understanding the love of the Father is the "meat" when it comes to developing a spiritual palate. Sometimes understanding that love means allowing God to unravel ideas and preconceptions. It might even entail learning what real love means. Understanding and accepting this love is the foundation of our faith. Whether we grew up going to church with our mother and father or we grew up fatherless, never stepping foot in a church, our childhood memories shape us. Our experiences influence how we view God the Father. Whether you were raised by the Father of the Year or a deadbeat dad, the Father's love for you surpasses all your experience of your earthly father.

My girls were raised on Disney movies. During one of Rielly's particular obsessions, I became very familiar with Disney's 1998 animated film *Mulan*. It really resonated with me. I loved how passionately Mulan cared for her dad and her family name. It drove her to disguise herself in a man's world while remaining true to herself. She had to work harder and longer than her peers. At one point during the film, Mulan sings a haunting song called "Reflection." Mulan pours out her heart in the song, admitting her fears about disappointing her family, wondering if she's losing herself in the attempt to save her family's honor.

At that moment, her father approaches her as she's looking at her reflection in a pond. He notices a flower that had not yet bloomed. Showing it to Mulan, he encourages her. "Look, a late bloom, and yet when it blooms, it will be the most beautiful of all."

God the Father is like this in His love for us. We struggle to understand or accept this type of unending love because we allow our life experiences to overshadow His love. In the Book of Isaiah, God tells us plainly that we won't always understand the ways of His love. He tells us that His ways are not our ways (Isaiah 55:8). If we try to project our own heartbreaks onto God, we will fail to truly grasp His love for us.

Higher Ways, Higher Love

When someone is grieving or walking through a particularly difficult unraveling, it's hard to know what to say. We walked through a season like this, and we heard a lot of "Christian-ese" from well-meaning people. People told us that God's ways are higher, that He would use this pain for His glory.

I wanted to punch them all in their pie holes. When someone is deeply suffering, reminding them of God's promises in this way is not always the most effective. And I'm guilty of doing this, too. When my girls are suffering, I turn to those lines of Scripture. I long to encourage them, but I know I just end up frustrating them. Thankfully, they call me out on it and call me to be a better companion.

God doesn't need us to defend His love for Him. God is big enough to do that on His own. He doesn't need me to play Holy Spirit or Bible Drill Master to others.

When it comes to the people we love, it's hard to take a backseat and let the Lord fill the space. This is especially true when it comes to us mommas. We want to take care of our babies, to defend them, to urge them onward. But God loves our babies immensely more than we do. To pretend otherwise is to offend Him. This is the heart of Isaiah 55:8. His ways are higher because His love is higher.

When we ask Jesus into our hearts, we take the first step toward believing in God's love. Roman 8:5 tells us that, while we were sinners, Christ died for us. For those of us who are justice-minded, this verse can be difficult to comprehend. But God's love claims us as His own, no matter what. When He died on the cross, He knew all about us. He knew all our yuck, our secrets, our sins, the ways we fail. God fully knows us. He wasn't tricked to get a treat.

"Above all, love each other deeply, because love covers a multitude of sins." –1 Peter 4:8

Let's pause and re-read 1 Peter 4:8. Rewrite it below in your own words.

Everything changes when we allow God's love to truly penetrate our hearts. The ability to allow God's love to unfold in our minds and take root in our hearts unleashes an unfathomable chain reaction. When we allow God's love to be the soil in our lives and allow Him to plant His love in our mind and hearts, a garden of goodness springs up.

Growing up, many of us raised in Christian churches heard a lot about the rules and regulations of God, but not so much about His mercy and love. We feared hell, but we didn't hope for heaven. While God does expect us to live in His ways, He is always ready to extend His mercy. Understanding this—understanding His heart—changes our entire faith.

If you're smothered in shame right now, it can be hard to embrace this type of unfailing love from the Father. But if you can give Him your shame, and let it rest at His feet, you will see Him move mountains to get to you.

Either way, the choice is up to you. Faith or doubt.

When it comes to the Father's love for you, do you have faith to believe it, or do you doubt that God could love you?

Why do you feel that way?

Doubt is a *decision*. Faith might feel impossible in this situation, but difficulty is just a dilemma. Difficulty is just a stage.

We can look at Scripture and find countless stories of how God's love covered bad choices in His children's lives. We can see that God's love isn't temporary or even conditional. We can see the thread of God's love sprinkled throughout His kept promise to Abraham. While we live in a society that sees love as a temporary sentiment that comes and goes based on our feeling-of-the-day, God's love is different. God's love is everlasting.

Nothing and No One

If we want to bust through the "barriers of life" that are keeping us from going to the next level with God, let's take a look in the life of Paul. Here, you have a guy who did a complete 180. He went from killing and persecuting Christians to being the most influential Christian. To make that type of change, he had to face some major skeletons in his closet. He had to allow God to unravel his former ways of thinking. He had to allow God to unravel the belief that He couldn't love him. Paul faced unthinkable hardship, from being stoned and beaten to being jailed and mocked. He went from being a heavy hitter on one team to being transferred to another.

Read what Paul writes in Romans 8:38-39:

"For I am convinced that neither death nor life, neither angels nor demons, neither present not future, or any powers, neither height nor depth, nor anything else in all creation, will be able to separate us from the love of God that is in Christ Jesus our Lord."

In this verse, what stood out to you the most about God's love for you?

Paul shot for that glass ceiling, the barrier we so often place over our minds and hearts to keep us from understanding God's love. Paul didn't want to leave anything uncovered. Did you get what he was saying in the verses above? *Nothing* and *no one* can separate us from God's love. Not even ourselves! Not even our thoughts. Now *that* is a different type of love.

Nothing and no one can separate us from God's love. Not even ourselves!

"The Lord appeared to us in the past, saying: "I have loved you with an everlasting love; I have drawn you with loving-kindness."" —Jeremiah 31:3

Read and rewrite Jeremiah 31:3.

I frequently remind my husband that he's my "person." I love him. He's my favorite human. Well, friend, *you* are God's person. His love for you is unchanging and everlasting. Nothing can or will ever take that away from you. So whether we are that late bloom, the one that is prettiest of all, or the gorgeous morning glory, we can rest in God's audacious love. He's ready to pour His love into our hearts in double and triple portions.

Let Us Pray

Lord, show me that my understanding of Your love is not what matters most. Help me believe that I am Your person. As I journey through my unraveling and any other painful moments in life, draw me closer to the truth of Your love. My hope is in You! My freedom is in You! My joy is in serving You, Lord. Amen.

Chapter 15

GOD'S TRACK RECORD

Trusting people isn't one of my top ten qualities, so learning to trust somcone I can't even see, especially when horrible things happen, can feel impossible.

Trust is a feeling or a general sense. Trust has to do with the way you or I perceive another person or source of information. If we trust someone, we believe that what they say is true.

When we believe someone, that belief is often based on individual facts and scenarios. Belief is garnered on a more case-by-case basis. Watch any nightly news segment. Reporters tend to say things like, "I believe that this country had plans to invade this other country, but I do not believe the president knew anything about it."

Trust and belief are two different things. But they go hand-in-hand.

So how do we learn to trust God when we aren't exactly the most trusting person? We look at His track record. Learning to trust God can be extremely difficult if your life is littered with betrayal. But if we want to develop our spiritual palettes and to be hungry for the desires of God, we have to be willing to try. Let's look at the God we confess, the God we say we trust. Let's look at His character and how He fought for Israel.

Sisters and Streetlights

Growing up, my little sister, Jamie, and I were partners in crime. I'm four years older, but she was my best friend. We fought like cats and dogs, but we defended each other to the point of blows. We knew we could trust each other.

Jamie and I loved being and playing together. We would come from school, rush through our homework, and hit the backyard. We would play basketball, throw the softball around, ride bikes around the neighborhood, or ride horses. What we did really didn't matter; we just wanted to be outside together.

We had the typical rules of kids in our day. We were allowed to play for hours on end until the street lights came on. When the street lights turned on, that was our signal to get home. And we'd better get home. Jamie and I knew we could always count on those street lights to warn us when it was time. They were trustworthy.

We can trust God to be our steady, guiding Light as we face times of uncertainty.

In Joshua chapters 9 and 10, we get a glimpse of the God we can trust. Joshua and the Israelites made a treaty with the Gibeonites. The Gibeonites deceived Joshua by dressing up and putting on the show of the century. They acted as though they were not part of the land Israel was inhabiting in order to avoid total destruction by the Israelites, as had happened with the King of Ai. Joshua entered into a treaty with them without first asking God.

The Israelites worked their way through the Promised Land, taking what the Lord had promised them. In chapter 10, the king of Jerusalem heard that Joshua had taken Ai and Jericho. Shaking in his boots, King Adoni-Zedek gathered four other kings. Together, they decided to work together to defeat Joshua.

First, they attacked the Gibeonites, the people who deceived Joshua. The Gibeonites got word to Joshua about the attack. The Lord then told Joshua to refrain from fear. He tells him that He has already delivered up the five kings to the hand of Israel. Joshua's trust is put to the test.

Scripture tells us that if we have faith the size of a mustard seed, we can overcome any and all circumstances. When we put that faith in the Lord, we trust and we believe that the Lord will handle whatever we face.

Joshua and his men marched all night to face the mighty army and took them by surprise. The Lord threw those armies and kings into great confusion. God hurled large hailstones from heaven that struck down only the enemy. When the Israelites were about to lose daylight, Joshua spoke to the moon and sun in the middle of battle. Talk about faith! God slowed the earth's axis, giving the Israelites enough time to complete the battle victoriously.

God is trustworthy. God keeps His promise. God never changes His mind, not one time. The same God who fought for Israel, despite all their mistakes, is the same God who fights for you. God is worthy of our trust. God's character is pure. God sees where you are, right now. He sees the hardships. The same God who hurled hailstorms at the enemies of Israel with such accuracy and precision is the same God who fights your enemies today. We can trust that, even in our unraveling process, God will use our struggles to remake us into beautiful creations. He will give us a story that will bring glory to His name.

Jesus came that we might have life; not just life, but *abundant* life. He achieved this by dying on a cross and rising from the dead. He unraveled the ways of the world and rebuilt it according to His ways.

What unraveling are you experiencing?

What temptation or hardship are you trying to overcome on your own?

There is no need to go at it alone anymore. Your Savior is fully capable and trustworthy. He can handle it all.

Who do you typically turn to for help in times of need?

You have an opportunity to trust the God of the Universe. Allow Him to unravel your way of believing and rebuild it into a solid foundation of trust. He is ready and willing to be your Provider, Savior, and Fighter.

We learn to trust the character of God by spending time in His Word, praying, journaling our prayers, and then watching His character remain the same. You have the victory, just like Joshua did, when you trust in God.

Let Us Pray

Lord, trusting You is hard. Help me to be content when things don't turn out the way I plan. Unravel my mind and remove any doubt in my heart. Lord, You brought the Israelites through war and devastation. You have proven Yourself trustworthy. Help me to take the steps today to see that You are the same God, worthy of my trust. Let it be done! Amen.

Part Four

UNRAVELING COMFORTABLE PATTERNS

The unraveling process is a lot like the sanctification process. The moment we ask Jesus into our hearts and declare Him Lord of our lives is the moment that the unraveling or sanctification process begins.

Sanctification refers to being set apart. When the Bible mentions someone or something being set apart, it is always through the sovereignty of God. As you flip from page to page, it is evident that God set apart people, places, and even days, each one with the same goal in mind: accomplishing God's plan.

We are set apart, sanctified, by being unraveled.

We are set apart, sanctified, by being unraveled. In this section, we'll learn how to adjust our lives and respond to God, allowing Him to work through us so we can accomplish His plans for our lives.

"So do not throw away your confidence it will be richly rewarded." –Hebrews 10:35

When we do the will of God, He rewards us. This makes our perseverance worth it. Once we decide to play an active role in the unraveling process, we place a stake in the ground. We choose to believe. We choose to have faith in God's character, to trust His promise.

133

In our joys and our struggles, we have a choice to make. We choose how we act.

We're all a part of a family, for better or for worse. Families can be difficult and amazing all at the same time. In our adult lives, most of us are trying to be better than our parents, to avoid making the mistakes that influenced our lives negatively, and to duplicate what our parents did well. As parents, we want to be better for our kids. We want their experience of family life to be better than our own. We have to know where we came from in order to improve going forward.

That is exactly what we are going to do. We are going to examine our "spiritual DNA."

Isaac, Rebekah, and their two sons, Esau and Jacob, had amazing spiritual DNA. Jacob's grandfather was Abraham. God had chosen this family and they were highly favored. But just because they were called and chosen didn't mean they weren't dysfunction junction.

In this section, we will strive to break some comfortable patterns that are passed down from generation to generation in our own families. Unraveling comfortable patterns is different from unraveling from sin, which we discussed in previous chapters. Once we unravel from major and habitual sin, the next phase is allowing God to unravel our comfortable patterns. Let's take a look at our hidden sin and comfortable patterns, facing them courageously.

Let Us Pray

Lord Jesus, unraveling with You is a process. Help me to fight for this freedom found in You. Help me to avoid discouragement or spiritual fatigue. Help me to stick and stay, right here with You. Bring me my breakthrough, Lord. Amen.

Chapter 16

SECRET SIN

The big fat "s" word. No one likes to talk, think, or hear about this word. Of course, I'm talking about *sin*. But we shouldn't shy away from the reality of sin. When we pretend sin doesn't exist, we can't address it. When we face it head-on, we allow God to unravel our sin and comfortable patterns. God can even use our poor choices, our sin, to turn us around and remake us.

Scripture tells us that Satan and his demons have one goal for our lives, our families, our friends, and our communities: sin and death. Scripture also tells us that it is for freedom that Christ has set us free. This is the freedom for which we were created. So stand firm!

Before we're ready to address our secret sins, we need to know our enemy. The devil understands that the entire Bible is God's Word and that it is true. He understands God's commands. He knows what pleases God and what doesn't. He's tricky and smart, and he knows our weak spots. Satan tries to convince us that our sin is acceptable since it "doesn't hurt anyone." Satan knows his time is limited, so he uses all his best tactics to steal, kill, and destroy us.

Two Men, Two Choices

We see this path to secret sin play out in the life of Achan in Joshua 7. Achan was among Joshua's men who took Jericho. He was a strong and capable soldier. Before the march on Jericho, God gave Joshua specific instructions about what the men were to take, and what they were to leave. Joshua relayed this message to the soldiers.

"But keep away from the devoted things, so that you will not bring about your own destruction by taking any of them. Otherwise you will make the camp of Israel liable to destruction and bring trouble on it. All the silver and gold and articles of bronze and iron are sacred to the Lord and must go into God's treasury." –Joshua 6:18-19

Once the walls of Jericho fell, the Israelites were likely on a high from their victory. Remember, these men and women had been wandering in the desert for forty years. They lived meager lives. The wealth of Jericho was foreign to them. The luxury was unlike anything they'd seen since Egypt. There's no doubt that this type of opulence captured their imaginations in the face of Israel's simplicity. It's easy to make excuses for them. After all, we would probably feel the same way.

But God had issued orders.

When no one was looking, Achan obtained a beautiful robe, some silver, and some gold for himself. No one saw. No one knew. So no one could blame him or hurt him. His secret sin was harmless. Right? Wrong. This decision cost Achan his life and the lives of those dearest to him.

A little later, Joshua was faced with his own choice. The Israelite army, feeling pumped from their victory at Jericho, decided to press onward through the Promised Land. Joshua sent spies to scope out the competition. The spies returned confidently, basically saying, "These dudes ain't got nothing on us. Send maybe 2,000 men—3,000 max—and they'll be able to handle it."

Without consulting God, Joshua did as his spies suggested. However, their enemies were larger and stronger than initially reported, and the Israelites lost thirty-six men that day, the rest fleeing in terror.

So we have two different men, making two different (bad) choices. Their responses tell us everything we need to know.

Immediately, Joshua fell to his knees before the Lord and begged Him for mercy and wisdom. I love God's response:

"What are you doing down on your face? Israel has sinned; they have violated my covenant, which I commanded them to keep. They have taken some of the devoted things; they have stolen, they lied, they have put them with their own possessions." –Joshua 7:11

God then instructs the whole nation of Israel to:

"Go, consecrate the people. Tell them, "Consecrate yourself in preparation for tomorrow; for this is what the Lord, the God of Israel says: 'That which is devoted among you, O Israel. You can't stand against your enemies until you remove it.'"" –Joshua 7:13

There is a two-fold message in this verse.

First, God addressed those hurt by the secret sins of others.

We stay with an unfaithful spouse out of obligation and sacrifice for our children. But that isn't why Jesus wants us to stay. He wants us to stay because of mercy, because the Gospel is a message of mercy and grace. Jesus told us that He came to heal the sick, for the well have no need of a doctor (Mark 2:17). What if, every time you talked to God, you felt an underlying resentment from Him because of what He sacrificed for you? Would that be very productive in your relationship?

The moment we elevate ourselves because of our heroic sacrifices in the face of secret sin of people in our lives, we aren't imitating Christ. In fact, we have fallen prey to Satan's mental war. Remember the parable of the man who was shown grace for his debt, and then turned around and punished the man indebted to him (Matthew 18:21-35)? Apply that parable to the person whose secret sin is influencing your life. God has shown you the greatest mercy. Will you not also show mercy?

Second, God addressed those who committed the secret sin.

Satan's best lie is that our secret sin isn't hurting anyone else. He tempts us to believe that because no one else sees or knows about our sin, it isn't *really* wrong. In Achan's case, even though he thought his sin was secret, 36 men died. Their families were heartbroken and he brought shame and ultimately death on himself and his entire family.

The Bible says that anyone who thinks they have no sin deceives themselves (1 John 1:8). Lets go to the Lord right now and ask Him to expose our secret sins, even those sins we are unaware of.

Lord, most gracious God, thank You for Your Mercy. You are a holy, righteous God. I am not worthy to even sit at Your feet, and yet You sent Your Son to die on the cross and suffer greatly for me so that I can be free and dwell with You forever. Show me where I desire wrong and cling to past habits. Please, bring to my mind any secret or unrecognized sin right now so that I may ask for Your forgiveness. Thank You for Your grace and mercy. Help me now to be courageous. Amen.

Satan's best lie is that our secret sin isn't hurting anyone else.

You are Victorious

Joshua was promised victory over Jericho. When we invite Jesus into our hearts, He makes us the same promise. We are promised victory over sin. Our old self passes away and we become new creations in Christ.

The Israelites had two choices: they could fight for the Promised Land, or they could continue to wander in the desert. They could believe, or they could back out.

What is something you desire victory over in your own life? Is there a sin you can't seem to escape?

God told Joshua that Jericho would be delivered into his hands. But Joshua still sent spies. We can't sit back and hope God magically removes the sin in our lives and the lives of others. We can't ask for deliverance from reading soft-porn stories all while picking up our Kindle and diving into the latest romance novel. We have to do our part!

If you have a secret sin in your life, you must first confess and bring that sin to light. Second, you have to remove the stumbling block. Then, you have to find a buddy for accountability. You can't do this alone. Satan knows your weaknesses too well. God is in the business of character-building, not comfort, and Satan is in the business of combat. So armor up, take his secret weapon away from him, and bring it to the light by telling a trusted friend.

When we allow sin to fester in our lives, we forfeit the blessing of God. Staying comfortable in our secret sin costs us immense blessing. It is time to stop and ask God for forgiveness, find a friend, and break the chains.

Let's pause for a moment and reflect on our approach to the battle of sin.

Are you boldly going before the Lord each day? ______________________

Are you entering His courts with thanksgiving and praise daily? __________

Are you asking Him to search you and try you daily and remove anything in your life that would keep you from Him? ______________________

The gravity of your sin doesn't matter. The thief on the cross next to Jesus was guilty. But he realized, as he hung, that he had a choice. He could cling to his pride, or he could cling to mercy. He didn't have the opportunity to be baptized or to do anything impactful with the short remainder of his life, yet Jesus spoke words of life and hope to him. He promised him victory. He promised him paradise. So don't give the enemy the last word. Don't let him have power over you for another minute. There is no sin that the Lord won't forgive when we ask Him. So give your sin to God. Ask Him to free you. And don't worry about whether or not His love for you will wane, because it won't.

Like the Israelites, we have a choice. What will you choose today?

Let Us Pray

Lord, addressing my secret sin stinks. Help me bring it to the light. Help me to confess my sins to You. I want You to heal me; I want to be whole. Give me peace and hope that You can and will remove this yoke of slavery. Thank You for releasing me from my secret sins! I praise You for the freedom You have brought to my life and I thank You in advance for the freedom You're producing in my heart now! Amen.

Chapter 17

GENERATIONAL BAD HABITS

We all have bad habits. Some we picked up from our parents and friends, others we have picked up along the way. However we obtain them, we tend to carry them around like an expensive purse. We make excuses for them and we even brag about them. We know that they're unnecessary, maybe even harmful, but instead of ditching them, we justify them. This reality is made very clear to me when I think about my daughters. Are these the habits I want to pass on to them? Is this the legacy I want to leave them?

The story of Jacob and Rachel is known as one of the Bible's best love stories. Before we can get to that love story, however, we have to examine how Jacob was raised.

Jacob's family had some dysfunction. Jacob was his mom's favorite, even though his brother, Esau, was the oldest. This caused tension between the brothers, and they definitely picked up some bad habits from their parents. Jacob and his mother conspired against Esau and manipulated Isaac into giving Jacob the blessing that was intended for Esau.

If your family is filled with scandal, betrayal, manipulation, power struggles, and control issues, you're in good company! Even God's chosen people dealt with these sufferings of a fallen world. There was hope for them; there is hope for us, too!

Once Esau discovered the betrayal, Jacob was forced to flee for his life. His mother sent him to a relative in order to find a wife. Along his journey, Jacob stopped at a well and laid eyes on Rachel for the first time. You could say it was love at first sight. He discovered that Rachel was the daughter of Laban, his mother's brother. Jacob and Laban made an agreement for the hand of Rachel: Jacob could marry Rachel after working for Laban for seven years. When Jacob completed his service, he cashed in on the deal.

However, on their wedding night, Laban tricked Jacob and gave him his eldest daughter, Leah, instead of Rachel. Jacob woke the next morning confused and angry that he had been manipulated. He reaped what he had sown.

Had Jacob's mom and her brother learned this habit of manipulation from their family of origin? They were both quick to deceive. Could this be a generational bad habit that changed the course of the lives of the people they loved?

Bless Our Hearts

We can often easily identify these habits or unhealthy behaviors in other's lives. In the South, we tend to dismiss these bad habits as simple character flaws. "Bless her heart," we say when referring to someone's destructive behavior. But we struggle to see our own shortcomings.

In fact, we often view these bad habits as unchangeable parts of who we are. We believe that it's just who we are and we won't be able to change it. But thanks to the cross, there are no comfortable patterns that inevitably keep us chained.

My parents owned their own business, and they worked hard to achieve success and provide for us. They instilled in us an unmatched work ethic. While this is good in many ways, there is also merit in work/life balance. Us kids? We're not so good at that. My sister owns her own incredibly successful business. But to this day, she jokes that when our mom calls her, she immediately starts working. She could never disclose to our mom that she was just watching Netflix or hanging out. No, we were raised to be hard workers, good employees, and good business owners. So she starts sending emails, even while on the phone with our mom, just so she can report that she's hard at work.

What was modeled for us as children is often the hardest to unlearn. Even so, we get a choice. We can choose to change, to break patterns, to detach from habits, and to form a new, solid foundation in Christ.

When I was a little girl, my papaw was really sick and in the hospital. A well-meaning family member of mine encouraged me to pray for his healing. She told me that if I had enough faith, he would be healed. So I prayed. And prayed and prayed. I prayed like his life depended on it because, in my young mind, it did. Then the day came. The doctors informed us that Papaw was not going to survive. I was crushed, not only over the loss of his life but over my perceived failure to save him. I hadn't prayed enough, or well enough, or "right" enough. It took years for me to unwind this faulty theology in my mind and heart.

Undoing and uprooting these behaviors, addictions, patterns of thought, and frames of reference that we inherit feels like an unachievable task for some of us. For others, we adopt the grit mindset and believe that we can change these behaviors on our own if we just work hard enough.

The Right Tools for the Job

When you are fighting a war, building a project, or playing a game, you need the right equipment. You wouldn't use a tennis racket in a baseball game. So when it comes to changing behaviors, actions, feelings, or addictions, we have to be ready to fight. And that involves having the right tools.

My husband and I met at a young age. We were instantly attracted to one another. We complimented one another and just really enjoyed spending time together. When we weren't together, we were on the phone. We had it bad. We got married and had kids. In the midst of doing life together, we discovered that we both had deeper issues that needed to be addressed. It was only when things got so bad that they could no longer be avoided, excused, or swept under the rug did we decide to do something about it. I had a lot of work to do on myself, and I'm grateful the formation of my new family forced me to face the unhealthy patterns of my family of origin.

The best way to eradicate comfortable patterns is to determine the opposite patterns. Ask yourself: what do I struggle with, and what are the opposite behaviors? For example, if you struggle with anger, the opposite would be peace. If you struggle with control, the opposite would be surrender.

In 2 Corinthians 10:3-4, Paul reminds us of our spiritual weapons. These weapons have the power to demolish strongholds and break down prisons. Remember, in Christ, we have the victory! Satan will try to keep us trapped in these negative patterns. When we turn ourselves and our struggles over to Christ, He will not allow us to taste defeat!

Are You Willing to Change?

To unravel the comfortable patterns in our lives, we must be willing to do these things.

First, we have to decide that enough is enough and that we want to change.

Second, we must run to the throne, not the phone! We must remember God's good character. He is trustworthy.

Third, we have to trust the promise of God. Romans 6:14 tells us that sin shall not be our master. No matter what sin has controlled you in the past, or how it controls you now, it shall not be your master, in the Name of Jesus. It may take two days or two decades to break free, but Christ has the final victory.

The new inheritance God has for you is worth the fight. It's worth the pain of change. Allow God to give you an Israel blessing

The new inheritance God has for you is worth the fight.

Below is a list of common strongholds and comfortable patterns. Spend some time with God and this list. Circle the areas that have a foothold in your heart and life. Then, we will invite the Lord to unravel these comfortable patterns.

ANGER	PERFECTIONISM	YO-YO DIETING	PAIN
SMOKING	MANIPULATION	TRUST ISSUES	DIVORCE
EATING DISORDERS	DESIRE FOR APPROVAL	POVERTY	INFIDELITY
UNHEALTHY BODY IMAGE	ALCOHOLISM	GREED	PORN ADDICTION
SOCIAL MEDIA ADDICTION	CONTROL	PRIDE	WORK ATTACHMENT
RETAIL THERAPY	LIVING THROUGH KIDS	HATE/ PREJUDICE	LACK OF INITIATIVE
SELF-RIGHTEOUSNESS			

Let Us Pray

Lord, I worship You today! I thank You that Your Word isn't void. Because of You, sin will not be my master. Lord, I confess that I have allowed myself to _______________________________. Yet today, Father God, I ask that You break _______________________________ off my life. I ask that You replace it with Your fruits of the Spirit. I ask that You give me the strength to change this pattern. Give me a specific Scripture verse to cling to concerning this area I am facing. Bring to my mind any strongholds that I am unaware of, Lord. Break the stronghold of _____________________ in Jesus' Name. Break if off myself, my kids, any future kids, and future generations. Amen!

Chapter 18

RUNNING

I was in the middle of my fifth consecutive load of laundry when my sister-in-law, Abbey, called. My babies were still babies, snoozing happily in their cribs. I was grateful to see Abbey's name pop up on my phone—I always love talking with her. She pushes me to be a better version of myself, and we have a great time along the way.

This particular day, Abbey was calling to inform me that she was going to run a marathon. This was an item high on her bucket list, so she would have done it with or without me. But I didn't want her to be alone! So I agreed, having no real idea that running a marathon actually meant running 26.2 miles.

Our husbands had little faith that we would follow through on our training. But week after week, we rose before the sun to train. Those weeks turned into months, comprised of weekend training days. We even had to raise money in order to be a part of the marathon. There was a lot riding on this. We worked hard. But I'll be honest, if Abbey wasn't waiting on me, there would have been many mornings in which running from training is the only running I would have done.

God Doesn't Ship in Two Days

When our life plans don't turn out the way we hoped, our instinct is to tuck and run, both mentally and physically. We develop this pattern at a young age. I got my first taste of the running game when I was in the first grade. At recess, I was informed that a boy in my class was going to try to kiss me during tag. I wasn't thrilled at this prospect, so anytime he came near me, I ran to the opposite side of the playground.

J.K. Rowling once stated that "Numbing the pain for a while will make it worse when you finally feel it."[1]

Running mentally and physically from hurt, pain, and even new opportunities can become a comfortable pattern for a time. But eventually, we reach the point where we can no longer outrun the pain. When we learn that running doesn't serve us well, we position ourselves to lighten our load and unpack our baggage. No more bandaids. We're ready to heal completely.

To fix the real issue and get to the bottom of our pain, we have to stop running and start untangling. We live in a society that is accustomed to instant solutions. Now, even two-day shipping is too long. This isn't the way God's kingdom operates. Running doesn't work because God sees us at every moment. Instant solutions aren't ultimately productive because we're not a simple item to be shipped.

Running from our pain ushers in self-doubt. Satan is the master of marketing. He loves selling his half-truths, especially when our souls are already fragile. When Satan tempts you to run from your problems or pain, he tempts you to run from yourself. Each time we believe this lie and try to run away, we lose a piece of who we are, of who we were created to be.

When we sprint from one church to another, or jog to a new job instead of staying put, we put stock in our imperfections rather than in God's goodness. When we dash in the opposite direction of our struggles, we rob ourselves of joy. We allow Satan and others to distract us from perseverance. We feel trapped instead of free, abandoned instead of accompanied.

Here I Am

One of the most amazing leaders of faith started his journey by running away. Moses ran away from Egypt (Exodus 2). One day, when Moses was grown, he discovered that he was a Hebrew adopted by Pharaoh's daughter. Curious about his people, he went forth from the palace to witness their slave labor. Moses saw an Egyptian beating a Hebrew. Moses killed the Egyptian in anger. Afraid of the consequences he would face, Moses left Egypt and began to run at age 40. He ran and ran until he rested at a well. As Moses was drawing water, he witnessed an incident between seven sisters and another group of men attempting to drive them away. Moses came to the sisters' rescue and watered their flock.

Moses married one of the sisters and moved to her land of Midian. They lived peacefully with her family. Moses became a shepherd. But when Moses was 80, God began to unravel him again. He called Moses to return to his homeland of Egypt, to face Pharaoh, and to lead his people to the Promised Land. Moses was content running, and he initially resisted this call. But we can only run so long and so far until we reach the end of ourselves. There, God is waiting with our destiny.

Once we discover that running isn't the answer to our suffering, we uncover the freedom found in surrender. Our destinies are revealed and launched through our pain and heartbreak. What the enemy tries to steal, we reclaim when we stop running. When we allow God to unravel our pattern of running, we place a stake in the ground. We embrace the Holy Spirit inside us and choose Him as our personal travel guide to freedom. Here, we find our purpose, just as Moses did.

Our destinies are revealed and launched through our pain and heartbreak.

"When the Lord saw that he had gone over to look, God called to him from within the bush, "Moses! Moses!" And Moses said, "Here I am."" —Exodus 3:4

When we are able to say, "Here I am," we position ourselves to receive God's healing, His will, and His freedom.

We can all relate to Moses in his initial resistance to God's request to return to Egypt. Sometimes, God asks us to do something difficult and we ask the same questions as Moses: "Why me?"

Where or what are you running from?

How long have you been running

How are you relying on yourself rather than God?

Where do you feel like a stranger or feel alone?

Where do you need to pause and say to God, "Here I am"?

Journal a prayer and confession of your running. Be real with God and tell Him about your fears, your hesitations, your questions. Ask Him to come to you, like He came to Moses in the burning bush, and reveal His will for this circumstance.

Like Moses, many of us come to our unraveling when we're running. If Moses hadn't stopped running, if he hadn't listened to God's call to revisit to a place of pain, the Israelites would not have been liberated and led to the Promised Land. What are we missing when we refuse to stop, when we refuse to heed God's call? Who remains captive because of our unwillingness to do the hard thing? Let's stand and not retreat. Let's receive and not ignore. Like Moses, let's remove our sandals during our unraveling, on this holy ground, and say, "Here I am."

Let Us Pray

Lord, help me to stand firm in knowing that You are the great I AM. You are the God of Abraham, the God of Isaac, and the God of Jacob. I can rest, knowing You are aware of the afflictions I face. I know that You are making a way. Help me to stand in Your promise and Your direction. I don't want to run anymore, Lord. I am here with You, ready to listen, ready to face, and ready to conquer through You. Amen.

Chapter 19

OUR RESPONSE WHEN WE DON'T UNDERSTAND

In Genesis 21, we see that God made good on His promise to Abraham and Sarah. Their son, Isaac, is born! Now remember, this wasn't technically the first child Abraham produced. After God revealed His plan to Abraham—the plan to give him a child in his old age—his wife, Sarah grew impatient. Things weren't happening fast enough for her and she grew desperate. Her self-made timeline was passing quickly, and she decided to play God. She took matters into her own hands. Can you relate?

We so often and so quickly grow tired of the waiting game. When we receive a promise, we are tempted to construct its fulfillment in our own minds. And we like our plan. We become attached to our plan. So when the pieces of our puzzle-plan don't fall like we think they should, we become frustrated and fed up. We don't understand. We think that the only solution available now, then, is to play God and do something about it ourselves. How often has that worked out well for you?

Sarah decided she'd waited long enough for God to act. She gave Abraham her servant, Hagar, and she bore him a son, Ishmael. Seems like a temporary solution to the problem. But it wasn't God's solution. Sometimes, when we step in, we get an outcome that appears to work. It can even feel like the perfect fit. But really, our interference just delays God's promise and makes temporal matters worse.

Hagar and Ishmael are often viewed as the villains in this story. But that's not how Scripture treats them. Abraham raised Ishmael as his own. He provided for Ishmael and Hagar. But once Isaac was born, Sarah grew weary of their presence and demanded that Abraham send them away. Abraham agreed and sent them into the desert, knowing their odds of survival weren't high. How painful this moment must have been! How confusing for Hagar and Ishmael. How hopeless.

How do we respond in seasons when we don't understand? How do we react when God seems cruel, when He seems to turn His back on us, to send us into the desert to die?

After time spent in the desert, Hagar's supplies ran dry and they were left with nothing. The time had come. Unable to bear witnessing her child perish, Hagar left Ishmael under a bush and walked away. Her heart must have been filled with doubt, for just a few chapters ago, God promised that He would provide for her and her son. Was she angry? Confused? Conflicted? I would have been.

Once we realize that our constructed plans are falling apart, we are in the position to be rebuilt.

Opening Our Eyes

As a mom, I really relate to Hagar. You can't raise three daughters and not walk through your fair share of heartbreak, helplessness, and horror. I've witnessed my child melt in the face of her demons, a solution seemingly nowhere in sight. It was almost unbearable to watch. Days felt like years as we tried to keep our sanity. I begged and pleaded with God. I tried bargaining with Him. I was willing to do anything to fix the problem for the child I love so dearly. Her unraveling became my unraveling. And through the process, God emptied me to make more room for Him. Nothing about this season felt good, even though He was working out my good. Hagar wasn't crazy and she wasn't cruel—she was a mom.

How will we respond when we don't understand? What are we going to do when God feels like an unjust God? What will we choose when we pray for change and nothing happens?

We're wired to believe that we need some conference or four-step plan to teach us how to feel and behave in these moments. But it doesn't work that way. Hagar came to the point where she sobbed and gave up. She had nothing left to give. Fear overcame her. She came to the end of her own abilities, her own ideas, and her own strivings. She could no longer function on her own.

That's the unraveling. And that's when God moves mightily.

In the desert, God heard Ishmael's cries. He sent an angel to Hagar to bring her hope. He promised that a great nation would come from Ishmael. Then, God opened Hagar's eyes, and she beheld a well of water.

In our unraveling, it can seem as though God isn't moving. In my particular unraveling, God was actually positioning my daughter to be able to cry out to Him herself. And God heard her, just as He heard me, and just as He heard Hagar.

Unraveling Our Swirling Thoughts

God wants to unravel our thoughts, our plans, our ideas, and our efforts so He can replace them with His own.

Trusting God and growing in intimacy with Him takes action on our part. We have to cry out. Of course, God sees our hearts. He sees past our masks and our "fake it 'til we make it." He sees our emotions and the feelings we hide from everyone else. He sees our desperation. But He wants us to invite Him into those places. Remember, we have a choice. We can run or we can rest; we can cower or we can fight; we can let Him in or shut Him out. When we cry out, He opens our eyes.

Our timing is not His timing. When we encounter delays, we need to remember those aren't God's denials. They are God's *decisions*. They are God's way of preparing to open our eyes. God does not hold back His purposes. We just have to be willing to wait with Him, even when we don't understand. We have to let Him open our eyes, even when we don't believe we can see.

> *When we encounter delays, we need to remember those aren't God's denials. They are God's decisions.*

Let Us Pray

Most gracious heavenly Father, as I watch someone I love dearly walk through their unraveling process, remind me of Your love for them. I naturally want to exchange places with them, and yet I can't. Thank You for sending Your Son and exchanging places with me. Thank You for pouring out your mercy on me. While I want to push the easy button, You are pushing the completion button. Help us all to hold on and trust You. Amen.

Chapter 20

HIS WAY IS BETTER

At the beginning of 2019, I, along with the rest of America, got swept up in the craze of *Tidying Up*. This Netflix series centered around the method and person of Kon Mari, an organizational wizard. This method encourages the purging and ordering of one's home. The litmus test for whether or not to keep a particular item is to hold it in your hands and to see if it sparks joy in your heart. If it does, it stays; if it doesn't, it goes.

I jokingly asked my friends, "What if everything I own sparks joy? Do I get to keep it all?!" Eventually, I set about clearing out my closest and drawers, snapping proud pictures of my perfectly-folded pajamas and sending them to my friends.

While the decluttering of my home initially felt like a huge process filled with mess and overwhelm, in the end, it was freeing. Everything in my home now has a place and a purpose. The same is true with life. Every season has a purpose and a reason. Some of those seasons are fun and overtly rewarding. Others are grueling and painful. Nevertheless, each season is designed to help us grow and mature into the person God created us to be.

Before we move deeper into the unraveling process, we have to understand some basic truths of Christianity so we can allow the process itself to "spark joy."

Jesus gave His life freely for you. He died so that, no matter what you have done or will do, you can be with Him. He died because He loves you despite the yuck in your heart. He wants nothing more than to be known and loved by You.

The moment we ask Jesus into our hearts, we give Him permission to use us, to change us, to unravel us. The process of purging might not always be fun, but He promises us everlasting joy in Him. It might be painful to say goodbye to certain possessions or patterns, but God is the Master Organizer. If that doesn't spark joy, I don't know what will.

Hospitals and Hope

My pregnancies were difficult. Each had their own unique trials, but they all left me on bedrest, fighting to survive. As weird as it sounds, I wouldn't trade those extended stays in the hospital for anything. Amidst the tubes and the wires and the unfamiliarity and the loneliness, God taught me great lessons of reliance.

One night in particular, I got tired of pushing the button that calls the nurse for help. Cort was gone, taking care of our other children and working his full-time job to pay for the hospital bills that were increasing by the minute. My hillbilly stubbornness took over. Weak and dehydrated, I felt the wave of nausea rise. I was determined to make it to the bathroom with my own strength, on my own time. On my own. I unplugged the IVs and stood up. Dizzy and sick, I barely made it to the bathroom without collapsing.

A glance in the bathroom mirror provided visual proof that my body was wasting away. My face betrayed my emotions—I had no strength left, no fight remained. Using the IV pole to steady myself, I sank to the floor next to the toilet. I desperately longed for my husband to be there, to help me and console me. I wanted his encouragement and his sympathy.

I brought my hand to my stomach, remembering the life within me. All I could think of was grace. Once again, I found myself pregnant, on the bathroom floor, alone. It was just me, this baby, and God.

As I stared up at the ceiling, a peace settled over me. I thought of how the Lord suffered when He gave His life for me. He was no stranger to feeling physically spent. He understood this pain of mine, and He met me in it. The conversations He and I had that night will forever be locked and cherished in my heart.

"For we know that all creation has been in groaning as in pains of childbirth right up to the present time. And we believers also groan even though we haven't the Holy Spirit within us as a foretaste of future glory, for we long for our bodies to be released from sin and suffering." —Romans 8:22-23

In the middle of the unraveling, we have hope because we are saved.

In Our Weakness

"And the Holy Spirit helps us in our weakness." —Romans 9:26

On the hospital floor that night, I truly understood this verse from Romans for the first time. It sank from my head to my heart. The Holy Spirit knows our every need, even when we can't properly articulate it. When we come to the end of ourselves, when we are in pain, it is the Spirit who prays and groans for us. We only need to stay in the game, ready to show up, ready to groan, and ready to release.

In the end, we can rest in knowing that God causes all things to work together for our good. We don't need to overthink it. We don't need to follow a particular procedure or method of prayer. All He asks for is our hearts.

The unraveling process can seem exhausting and endless. So rest in this truth. God is always intentional. In the beginning, before God created the earth, He hovered over the water. His hovering was intentional, and this became clear when He said, "Let there be light!" and there was light. God knew creation would be a process. And He knows that our new creation, our unraveling, is a process. He is more than ready to sustain us through that process. Just as He was intentional in creating the world, so too is He intentional in recreating us. He hovers over those places in our lives that are painful. He hovers over our hardships, taking His time, being intentional with every movement. He has a beautiful plan for our unraveling.

God is transforming us to be more like His Son. He is making us more like Jesus. Jesus went before us in His own unraveling process. Of course, He didn't need an unraveling process for Himself. He was perfect. But in His love for us, He lived the unraveling process to show us the way. He knew we would need His example. He chose us and called us to be His witnesses, and the unraveling process will ultimately tell of His glory.

Just as He was intentional in creating the world, so too is He intentional in recreating us.

Isn't this what made the suffering of Paul worth it to him? He had a taste of the glory awaiting him, so he faced his own pain, suffering, and betrayal with true joy sparked in his heart.

God expects us to unravel because He Himself unraveled when He gave Himself for us. This is the way of Christ. This is what it means to be a follower of God. I know this truth isn't popular in many Christian churches today, but we won't come out of any devastation retaining our faith if we don't accept it.

He will transform our moaning and sorrow into joy. His Word is filled with promises that we will face hardship, but that He will never leave us in the midst of it. We may feel as though we're pressed to the gates of hell itself, but Jesus is victorious.

The joy of unraveling is found in the process. The pain won't produce a worldly, fleeting happiness, but the presence of God in the middle of our most intense storms brings joy where there is sorrow. He brings light where there is darkness. If you feel dizzy from your sufferings—sprawled on your back on a bathroom floor in a hospital gown that reveals too much of your backside—look up. Look up to heaven and remember that Jesus went through the unraveling process for you. He holds you now during yours.

Let Us Pray

Jesus, I am tired and exhausted. I am plagued by my circumstances. Nevertheless, I trust in You. I know that it will be worth it. I know that You are bringing about a new song and new hope, even now. Help me to choose joy. Give me willpower beyond my power. Help me to hold fast to Your Word. Deposit grace and joy in my life. Let Your mercy overflow so that I can't help but sing of Your goodness. Thank You for leading and guiding me. Amen.

Part Five

JOY IN THE UNRAVELING

Before we can experience authentic joy during our unraveling, we have to understand what joy really means. Joy is not the same thing as happiness. During my seasons of unraveling, I didn't experience much superficial, emotional happiness. Joy is something deeper. It's undeterred by circumstance or emotion. Most importantly, joy is a *choice*.

Recently I received a traffic ticket for a violation I wasn't convinced was fair. I presented myself in court, and instantly I felt like I was fighting a losing battle. The traffic judge humiliated me. The entire courtroom—including the judge—laughed at my expense. Those in power used that power to belittle me for a few laughs. Normally, this kind of embarrassment wouldn't bother me, but I was so upset over the outcome and their behavior that I was completely undone. My sweet daughter, Kailee, encouraged me as we left the courthouse. "Mom, you have a lot of good things going on right now. The enemy is trying to steal your joy!"

In that moment, I couldn't choose joy right away, and that's okay. Even though I am confident in God's Word and truth, sometimes I just have an empty tank. I was hit with disappointment and discouragement. My world felt like it was crashing down. So I retreated to my quiet place—the shower—and soaked in the water and silence as tears soaked my face.

A hymn from my childhood started to play over and over in my mind. "It Is Well with My Soul" by Horatio Spafford and Philip Bliss welled up within me and brought me comfort. I was spinning out, and the truth in this hymn brought stillness.

No matter what we face, we can rest knowing that our faith, trust, belief, and chosen joy lies in Jesus.

———————————

King David gives us the perfect example of what it looks like to be joyful in the midst of unraveling.

Throughout the psalms, David cries out to God for help. He gets real and gritty with God. He doesn't hold back. David is very clear about his suffering. He feels alone, abandoned, unheard, and defeated. He begs God to rescue him, and all he hears is silence. Ever felt this way? None of us get through life without having a Psalm 88 moment (or twenty). Psalm 88 is a long psalm, and I encourage you to read it all. But just to paint the picture, the psalm ends with this line:

"You have taken from me friend and neighbor—darkness is my closest friend."
—Psalm 88:18

David was in deep.

But look at the next chapter, Psalm 89. David goes on to praise the Lord for His unfailing love! David decides to declare his adoration despite his disappointment! That is what it means to choose joy in the midst of unraveling.

Inside Out

"Consider it pure joy, my brothers and sisters, whenever you face trials of many kinds, because you know that the testing of your faith produces perseverance. Let perseverance finish its work so that you may be mature and complete, not lacking anything."
—James 1:2

We can't rely on our moods. Our moods are fleeting and faulty. We have to choose to persevere despite how we feel. James wrote this verse to people who were being persecuted for their faith. They were forced to leave their homes, to run for their lives, to forsake family and community. *That's* real suffering. So James wrote this to encourage them, to remind them that there is still joy in their lives despite the destruction.

In the Pixar movie *Inside Out*, we step inside a child's mind and become acquainted with all her emotions. She sorts through Joy, Anger, Fear, Disgust, and other emotions we all feel. In the end, Joy and Sadness come together, and the little girl experiences a bittersweet memory for the first time.

This is James' message. While we might feel sad in the moment (and rightly so), we are called to consider it joy, knowing that God is always good and that He never leaves us.

Unraveling is a lot like learning how to budget for the first time. We overdraw a few times and we discover all the secret fees. But slowly, with effort, we begin to understand how we spend our money and any necessary adjustments become evident. Pretty soon, we become masters of our money instead of our money lording over us. There's freedom and empowerment there. So while unraveling is uncomfortable and frustrating, the purpose pushes us forward to a greater fulfillment.

I don't have to tell you that life isn't always filled with unicorns and rainbows. You've already tasted bitterness, I'm sure. But I can tell you this with certainty: we can face our most difficult circumstances with joy, knowing that God is going to use them to rebuild us and to create something amazing.

We have three choices in life:

Choose Joy
Stay Still And Be Wishy Washy
Choose Anger

If we dare go "all in" and choose complete joy, we are freed from the grip of the enemy. The evil one can't hold us captive in our unraveling.

So what will you choose? How will you approach your unraveling? Will you choose to be released from bondage? Will you choose joy?

Allow joy to protect, empower, and guide you. If we can get this mindset right, if we can live in the bittersweet, our lives will become a harmonious testimony, proclaiming all is well.

> If we can live in the bittersweet, our lives will become a harmonious testimony, proclaiming all is well.

Let Us Pray

Lord, today I don't feel like choosing Your complete joy. I would rather chew on my pain and stay put. But I know that would delay my unraveling. My circumstances feel so heavy. Everyone around me is bringing me down. I feel like I am drowning. Every time I take a breath, a wave of doubt, hate, and anger knocks me under. Help me hold my breath and choose Your complete joy as life unravels me. Help me declare Your goodness. Thank You for Your patience with me. Help me extend that grace to others. Help me exchange my anger and pain for Your laughter and joy. Amen!

Chapter 21

YOUR ANSWERED PRAYERS

Zechariah was a priest. He knew the Scrolls backwards and forwards. He knew all about the God he served. But his faith hadn't yet sunk from his head to his heart when we see him in Luke 1. We don't often have a heart-conversion experience until we really encounter God for who He is, not just what He know about Him.

Let's take a look at Zechariah's unraveling experience and how God counters objection from Zechariah. We'll see how God used Zechariah's unraveling to bring about his wholeness and joy.

Zechariah was from the priestly order of Anijah. His wife, Elizabeth, was a direct descendant of Aaron, Moses' brother. They obeyed God's laws, and God affirmed their righteousness (how cool would that be?!). Elizabeth and Zechariah longed for a child, but much like Abraham and Sarah, they were advanced in years. In the eyes of the world, their situation looked bleak.

But 400 years before, God made a promise to Israel. He promised a Savior, a Redeemer. And He was preparing to fulfill it.

In Luke 1, we encounter Zechariah at work in the temple, performing his basic priestly duties. Let's pause here. Zechariah is about to have a major, life- and world-changing encounter with God, right in the midst of his daily tasks. God often works His miracles in the midst of our simple, mundane daily duties. Rarely do we experience flashy moments of revelation; but the Lord is always ready to fulfill His promise over our lives while we simply remain faithful to our duties.

Is there a time in your life when God spoke life or worked through your regular daily tasks?

On this particular day, Zechariah was chosen to be the one priest to enter the Holy of Holies. This was a big deal, a great honor and privilege, an opportunity that didn't come around every day. So Zechariah went before the Lord while a large crowd stood outside, waiting and praying. Zechariah received the shock of his lifetime when he turned to the right of the incense altar and saw Gabriel, the angel of the Lord.

God often works His miracles in the midst of our simple, mundane daily duties.

Gabriel quickly realized that Zechariah was afraid and overwhelmed, so he assured him, "Do not be afraid, Zechariah! God has heard your prayer. Your wife, Elizabeth, will give you a son, and your are to name him John" (Luke 1:13).

Gabriel promised Zechariah great joy and gladness, revealing that many would rejoice at the birth of the boy, for he would be great in the eyes of the Lord. What a massive calling upon the lives of Zechariah and Elizabeth! They were righteous, but not perfect. Zechariah, knowing the Scriptures, would have understood the significance of this promise. This moment was weighty.

Gabriel continued to instruct Zechariah on how to raise this promised son. He revealed that this offspring would be God's messenger, preparing the way of the Lord. Instead of accepting this message of hope and salvation, Zechariah doubted. He reminded Gabriel of his old age, and of Elizabeth's inability to bear children. His mind left no room for the miraculous. Zechariah unraveled.

When Zechariah exited the temple, he was met with the confused gaze of the crowd. What had taken so long? Zechariah was unable to explain what happened because the Lord removed his ability to speak. He attempted to make gestures to recount the events and the promise. Here, we have the first documentation of the game of charades.

Zechariah went home to Elizabeth, eager to "tell" her the news. Can you imagine hearing this, as Elizabeth? Like Sarah, she lived her life in shame and confusion, wondering why she was unable to bear children. What a message of hope this was for her! And she received it with joy and confidence. Soon afterward, Elizabeth became pregnant. She praised the Lord for taking away her shame and showing her favor.

It's interesting to note the differences in how Zechariah and Elizabeth responded. They were both righteous people and they both sought God, even in the midst of their struggles. But facing the same unraveling, one rejoiced and the other doubted. Elizabeth wow'd it to life, while Zechariah how'd it to death.

How will you receive the answer to your prayer? When you come to the end of yourself, when you unravel, how will you respond? Will you question, steeped in your cynicism? Or will you trust, knowing the character of your Creator and rejoicing in His ability to make the impossible possible?

The Faith of Little Children

Our daughter, Kailee Grace, has a relationship with the Lord that greatly inspires me. She has a thirst for growing in God. While most kids are watching YouTube or jamming to music all night, Kailee stays awake, reading over Scripture. She has unshakeable faith.

Once while my husband was away on a business trip, Kailee started to feel ill. She went down fast with the flu. But as she crawled onto the couch, where she would remain for a few days, she was claiming healing in Jesus' Name. She looked pale and lethargic. She told me she was fine, but I'm her momma, and I could see it in her eyes. She was hurting. I told her, "Baby, you can expect God to heal you *and* still let Mom know how you're really feeling."

She looked at me, assured, and said, "Mom, I am just waiting on my healing. It's coming!"

Kailee didn't let her circumstances determine her attitude. She went through her own small but significant unraveling, and she chose faith. She chose joy. She clung to the promise of God and did not doubt His ability to heal her. She stood on her trust and persevered through the aches and pains. Kailee declared healing despite her feelings.

I wish I had her faith.

How can you increase your faith?

Think of an unraveling you're going through right now. What will you claim, in Jesus' Name, over this hardship?

What promises of God do you need to "wow to life" instead of "how to death"?

Walking through difficulties is never fun. But the way we walk through them either sets us up for a comeback, or sets us back for another go-around. When we can persevere through trials, we place God's will and way over our own. We don't get a comeback without collapses. We don't get a breakthrough without a breakdown. We don't get resurrection without death.

How would your sufferings transform if you chose joy and claimed victory in the Name of Jesus?

Let Us Pray

Lord, my help comes from You. Help me to know that You are carrying me on Your shoulders. In my sickness, my pain, and my brokenness, You show up. Help me to declare Your fidelity and Your mercy. Where I see a setback, Lord, You see a set up. Help me to turn my suffering into a tool of transformation. Help me to choose joy and claim victory in Your Name, Jesus. Amen!

Chapter 22

STEP BY STEP

I love music, all kinds of music. Give me a beat and I will tap my feet and sway my hips. I find solace in music during hard times, joy in victory moments, and solidarity in the I-don't-know-what-to-do moments.

No one in our family plays an instrument, we do love to karaoke. In fact, our Christmas tradition revolves around it. Every Christmas Eve, we go to the church service, come home to unwrap matching family PJs, and enjoy a tailgate of Jesus' birthday party food. Then, we sing our hearts out along to our favorite jams. We all think we're Grammy-award winning artists.

But when Whitney Houston's "Step by Step" comes on, everyone clears the floor. This is my anthem, and they pass the mic to me.

I belt along with Whitney:

"Well there's a bridge and there's a river that I still must cross
As I'm going on my journey
Oh, I might be lost

And there's a road I have to follow, a place I have to go
Well no one told me just how to get there
But when I get there I'll know
Cuz I'm taking it

Step By Step, Bit by Bit,
Stone By Stone (Yeah), Brick by Brick (Oh, yeah)
Step By Step, Day By Day, Mile by mile (ooh, ooh, ooh)."[1]

I sing this song like it's the fight round on *The Voice.*

God has used this song to propel me forward in so many unraveling moments. This song carried me through my teenage pregnancy, and it keeps me going now.

Steady as We Grow

God does things in our lives step by step, little by little, inch by inch. We can become frustrated when things we want to happen quickly seem to crawl at a snail's pace. In these moments, we can be tempted to adopt an "all or nothing" mentality.

I am either the Rookie of the Year in Real Estate, or I am nothing. I am either completely debt free in a year or less, or I am a failure. I am either mom-of-the-year, or a negligent mom. I'm either a gourmet cook, or completely useless in the kitchen.

It's hard for me to accept that growth takes time. It's hard for me to accept good-enough instead of perfect.

God moves steadily, and He always wins the race.

Our culture has sold its soul to this idea. Everything has to be instant or it isn't worth it. We have to be the absolute best, or no one will care about us. We have to stay at home to be good moms while also becoming the next diamond rank in the next big company. We have to do it all and have it all. And we have to do and have it right now.

But God moves steadily, and He always wins the race.

"The Lord your God will drive those nations out ahead of you little by little. You will not clear them away all at once, otherwise the wild animals would multiply too quickly for you. But the Lord your God will hand them over to you. He will throw them into complete confusion until they are destroyed." –Deuteronomy 7:22-23

Here, we meet the Israelites as they've been wandering in the desert for 40 years under Moses' leadership. They're tired of walking. They're tired of hoping. They're grumpy. And they are tempted to give up. In this verse, we see Moses attempting to encourage the Israelites. He reminded them that the land they were about to enter is the Promised Land, the very land guaranteed them by the Lord.

Moses told the people that, with the help of God, they would clear away many nations: the Hittites, Girgashites, Amorites, Canaanites, Perizzites, Hivites, and Jebusites. Let's just call these seven nations the "ites" because those names are just too hard to say.

Moses reminded the people that all of this would happen little by little. If the Israelites took on too much too quickly, it would usher in their demise. But God is faithful and steady, and He had a plan for their victory. Moses reminded the Israelites that God was with them and that He would fulfill His promise. The entry into the Promised Land would not be instant, but it would be worth it.

The same is true for us during the unraveling process. When God fulfills His promises, it takes time. It takes time to unravel and remake us. He uses the step-by-step, little-by-little process to reveal the joy and build our testimonies.

Terrible Dinners and Divine Deliverance

Cooking has never been my thing. Yes, I am southern and love to wear aprons. And yes, my idea of cooking from scratch is pulling a carton out of the fridge and heating it up.

One night, in an effort to be more skilled in the kitchen, I decided to make my family a huge Mexican feast. I always take pride in setting the table, so while my dish baked, I put time and effort into a stunning table-scape. I carefully arranged the dishes and silverware and wrote individual place cards that included specific affirmations for each member of the family. I wanted this meal to be special.

When it was time to eat, I proudly presented my creation. Each family member took their serving and we prayed. As I got up to grab a drink, my family took their first bites of my creation. My husband looked at me, his eyes sparkling. "Is something wrong, baby?"

He smiled and said plainly, "Just waiting for you to try it!"

I returned to the table immediately and took one bite. I desperately wanted to stay committed to my dinner, to my pride-and-joy of the evening. But I can't hide a single feeling from my husband. Chaise announced flatly, "How about Taco Bell instead?" We all roared with laughter, knowing that Taco Bell sounded like a 5-star restaurant compared to what we just tasted.

Now, I could have let this setback ruin my taste for cooking forever. But I'm determined, and I wanted to grow my skill in this area. So for the last two years, I have hosted Thanksgiving dinner for my side of the family. The first year wasn't great, and it's still not perfect. But with time and practice, I have mastered the timing and execution of several dishes. I still have to outsource the turkey and ham, but someday, with little-by-little progress, I hope to cook my own turkey.

Just as God told the Israelites that He would deliver the Promised Land into their hands slowly for their protection, He tells us the same during our unraveling. God is delivering your story to you. But you can't handle it all at once. If you try to tackle it instantaneously, you'll grow weary and defeated. He only moves us, unravels us, and remakes us step by step.

Stop and reflect. What has God brought you through in the past? From where has He brought you?

Are you in the middle of unraveling right now? It can feel endless and void of progress, but what are the little ways the Lord has moved so far?

In what ways have you found joy in the process?

How has the Lord worked in your life in small steps?

Rewrite this verse from Romans in your own words:

"May the God of hope fill you with all joy and peace as you trust in him, so that you may overflow with hope by the power of the Holy Spirit." –Romans 15:13

Let Us Pray

My Abba, my heavenly Father, my Comforter, my Deliver, Your heart beats for me. There is a reason why You have me cross these bridges. You have a plan, and Your plan is for my good. Help me to hear Your voice in the silence. Help me see You in my mistakes. God, help me to fix my eyes on You in my heartache. Help me to take steps toward healing. Refresh me. Help me choose joy in every step and in every situation. In the Name of Jesus, I pray this over my life today! Amen.

Chapter 23

NOW AND THEN

I stood on the balcony of our beautiful resort in Punta Cana, looking over the ocean. My family was still sleeping, and I had stepped out to take a business call. Most people would be annoyed by receiving a business call while on vacation, but not me. This business was the reason my family was able to go on such a luxurious vacation. I worked hard, I built something from nothing. And in my mind, our family had *arrived*.

After my call, I listened to the steady waves. My breath matched their rhythm. Then, God gave me my orders. "It's time, Tiffany. I am waiting on you. We have been through so much. It's time for you to retire your real estate license and do what I have called you to since you were young."

I knew exactly what He was referring to, but I wasn't about to give in that easy.

"What, God?! But I'm doing great! And now You want me to give it all up? I want to obey You, but look at our life! I make good money, and I give good money. And my family is able to enjoy moments like this!"

For months, I wrestled with this call. Finally, I decided to bring it to my husband. If anyone could talk some sense into me, it was Cort. I expected him to encourage me to follow God's call, but also maintain a part-time business. That's a solution I could envision. I could still sell houses, but also write and speak like the Lord asked. So I told Cort all about my conversation with God and how He told me it was time to speak and write. I quietly mentioned the part about retiring my business, and *really* emphasized the fact that we would be making virtually no money as a result. I waited for his reaction, confident that he would find a solution that would allow me to half-way obey.

"Revelation 3:16," was his only response.

I rushed to grab my Bible, looked up the verse, and read it aloud to us.

> *"So, because you are lukewarm—neither hot or cold—*
> *I am about to spit you out of my mouth."*

I didn't need to read any further. I didn't need Cort to explain what he meant. I knew exactly what he was insinuating. He knew exactly what this meant for our family. God wanted my complete and total buy-in.

For the sake of emphasis, I kept on reading.

> *"You say, "I am rich; I have acquired wealth and do not need a thing.""*
> *–Revelation 3:17*

Ouch. I knew immediately that the Holy Spirit was speaking to me through this verse. I remember the excuses I gave Him in Punta Cana. We were *comfortable*. I didn't want things to change. I didn't want to step into this new season. I was complacent. I was lukewarm.

A Peter Kind of Passion

In the Gospels, Peter is the unelected leader of the disciples. He was one of the first disciples who chose to follow Jesus. He is one of the three of who I would classify as Jesus' best friends. Peter was an all-in kind of guy. He was loud and proud. One of my favorite stories about Peter illustrates this fact (John 13:2-11).

In this account, Jesus is washing the feet of the disciples, a task typically reserved for servants. Remember, everyone wore sandals back then and the roads were dusty. I bet feet were super gross. When Jesus got to Peter, he refused the gesture. C'mon, man, who turns down a free pedicure?!

Jesus assured Peter, telling him that he didn't yet understand. But Peter continued to refuse, claiming that he was unworthy. Finally, Jesus said to Peter, "Unless I wash you, you have no part in me."

That got through to our stubborn leader, and he replied, "Not just my feet, but my hands and head!"

When Peter was asked a question, he immediately answered. When a problem presented itself, Peter was quick to offer a solution. He was sometimes seen as insensitive and immature, but Jesus chose him to be a leader and builder of His church.

Peter's unraveling came shortly after the feet-washing incident. When Jesus told the disciples He was leaving, Peter would not accept it. He proudly proclaimed that if Jesus was killed, he would be killed alongside Him. Peter's passion was palpable, and it propelled him to make this promise.

We know what happened next. Once Jesus was arrested, Peter denied Him three times, just as Jesus prophesied. He carried that deep sorrow and shame with him until he encountered Jesus after the Resurrection.

The Hardest Person to Forgive

Peter probably never fully forgot his betrayal of Jesus. I imagine that every time he heard a rooster crow, he wanted to throw that thing up against the barn. His passion never left him, even in his unraveling. Throughout his unraveling process, Peter probably began to understand that life had a brand new meaning. But fear tried to rob him of the joy of taking the next step into his new mission. Through the rest of the Gospels and New Testament, we see how God used Peter's unraveling to make him more fully himself. Peter became a great missionary, even giving his life for Christ, just as he said he would. But this time, he didn't chicken out.

We're not that different from Peter. God desperately wants to ignite our unraveling process so He can fulfill His best plan for our lives. But it can be scary. In the midst of the silence and bleakness of unraveling, we might wonder what good could possibly arise. Perhaps we've tried everything, worked every potential solution, and still come up with nothing. In this moment, we come to the end of ourselves. We come to the end of our passionate proclamations. We come to the end of our own strength and power and are left only with the power of God's promise.

> We come to the end of our own strength and power and are left only with the power of God's promise.

Even with all his flaws, Peter was a man who desired to be used by God. I have so much Peter in me. How about you?

Peter's character was unraveled from being self-focused to Jesus-focused. Jesus met Peter at the end of himself and allowed His truth to change Peter.

We get a choice. The truth can either help us or hurt us. Forgiving ourselves, like Peter had to do after his denial, is one of the hardest things we have to do. We forgive others more readily than we forgive ourselves. We believe that others are more worthy of kindness and compassion, even in their failings. But we don't extend the same grace to ourselves. That's another win for Satan. This half-truth can steal our joy, dampen our passion, and distract us from moving forward into God's call on our lives.

Jesus needed Peter to get out of Peter's way. He needs us to do the same.

Where in your life do you need to give yourself a break and a dose of compassion?

Where are you experiencing frustrating silence in your life?

Take some time to journal a prayer about your unraveling. Tell Jesus what might be holding you back. Consider how you might be getting in your own way. Surrender your Peter-like passion to Jesus so He can use it to build the kingdom.

Amen!

Let Us Pray

Lord, I am allowing my weakness to hold me back. I feel unqualified for what You are calling me to do. I feel like no one wants to hear my words or my story. I am allowing pride and stubbornness to paralyze me. Help me to get out of my own way. Help me to forgive myself as You forgive me. Speak to my spirit and remind me that You want to use me in a mighty way. Help me to surrender my Peter-like passion to You so that You can truly use it for Your glory. Amen!

Chapter 24

WRITE IT OUT TO RIDE IT OUT

I began to journal my prayers shortly after Cort and I were married. I needed to write my prayers; it was like therapy. Cort and I were in a legal battle involving my daughter. It's difficult to describe the pain we were steeped in as newlyweds, to detail the unspeakable pain of being betrayed by your closest family, to walk out a drama and a trial so publicly. It sucked the air from my lungs.

We felt like Gideon in Judges 6. The Amorites were oppressing the Israelites. God sent his angel to Gideon to relay a message of coming triumph. God told Gideon that He was going to help him raise up an army to defeat the Amorites. It was an impossible task. Gideon questioned the angel, asking why God let their oppression happen if He was really with them all along?

Oh, how we could relate. Cort and I were barely making ends meet, and now we needed to hire an attorney. We would have to file for bankruptcy before our first wedding anniversary if something didn't change quickly. I was angry with God. I couldn't understand why He allowed this to happen to us. It was difficult to praise when I felt paralyzed. The only way we moved through that season was through a simple decision.

The Bible talks about two paths: one is wide and easy, the other narrow and difficult. By God's grace, Cort and I chose to walk the narrow, unpopular path. While it looked to the world that we were defeated and while those who opposed us prospered, we kept our eyes fixed on the Lord. We chose to believe that He is good and faithful, even though our circumstances seemed to illustrate the opposite.

Now that we are on the other side of this particular unraveling, I can see God's hand in the midst of our overwhelming pain and fear. I could see

Gideon's success over the Amorites. I could see God's plan in his life and in our lives. The journey there didn't make sense, but God uses the good and the bad to unravel us and make us whole in Him.

During the trial, I penned this prayer:

Lord, I know You know I know You can do this, but there is something that keeps trying to pull me back. I am completely uncomfortable. I am afraid. I don't understand why You chose me to walk this when You can very easily change this with one word. Can I trust You God? Can I trust that You are really going to bring me through this? I am very angry! Anger fills my soul. Deliver me from the fears of the unknown. Lord, give me a chance of joy!

These emotions were raw and real, and God met me right there. Cling to your heavenly Father! He is big enough to handle your anger, your cuss words, your tears, and your punches. He is ever-patient, and He gives us a choice. We can stuff our fears and feelings and walk the wide way of the world, or we can empty our hearts before Him, offering the good and the bad, and cling closely to His side as we walk the narrow way.

A Forewarning

A week before our wedding, Cort and I attended a worship service at a non-denominational church. In the middle of worship, the guest speaker stopped the music, looked at me, and said, "Would you mind coming up here to pray over the congregation?"

My 20-year-old self was not quite comfortable with this yet. But I didn't want to be viewed as a coward! I figured I could mumble a prayer into a microphone for a couple hundred people. How bad could it be?

I walked on stage and accepted the microphone from the speaker. I closed my eyes, imagined that wind was blowing through my hair for dramatic effect, and talked to God as if we were the only two in the room. After I finished, I returned the microphone and began to walk back to my seat.

But the guest speaker stopped me. He said, "Pastor, do you mind if I speak a word I feel the Lord has for her and her husband?" Our pastor paused for a moment (likely considering the fact that Cort wouldn't be my husband for another week!), then agreed.

Eyes locked on mine, the speaker said, "The Lord has a spiritual baton. It's an anointing. The only way I can describe it is by likening it to the anointing that Joyce Meyer walks in."

"Great," I thought to myself. "Who is Joyce Meyer? Hope she's successful!"

Then the speaker dropped the word we all dread accompanying a compliment or good news…*but*.

"But you are both about to walk through hell and back. The Lord said you need to dive into the Word, and let it refine you and remake you."

Well, awesome. Nothing like receiving a word about walking through hell and back in front of a crowd the week before your wedding! I was sure we'd make new friends easily now with this target on our backs. But he wasn't finished.

"Brothers and sisters, this couple is going to need your support! They are an earth-moving couple in God's kingdom, but hell is coming after them."

I stood dazed and mostly confused. Was there a kink in this man's reception, delaying his connection to God? I had *already* been through hell and back. I had a kid at 17. Cort and I cancelled our initial wedding when our pastors expressed their concerns about our readiness. Hell had come and gone. Now we were getting married with our pastors' blessing. Now we were going to be a family. Now was our time to prosper.

But the guest speaker was right. On our honeymoon, Cort and I received a call that ushered in the greatest unraveling of our lives. Over the next several years, we walked through court cases, marital issues, counseling, long-term illness, and two unexpected pregnancies while Cort was both a full-time student and employee. We moved to two different states. Nothing was comfortable or familiar anymore. Hell raged war, but that guest speaker's word helped us cling to the sword of the Spirit.

We immersed ourselves in Scripture. We faced our long-suffering with the hope of redemption. We were in a battle for our futures, our destinies, and our future generations. We knew we weren't strong enough to face these trials on our own. God's truth resounded in our hearts through the hills and valleys. His Word kept us company when we felt completely alone in the world. He used us to inspire others, even in the middle of our desert. He brought us a joy that would baffle the rest of the world. And He fulfilled His promise, bringing purpose, peace, and glory from the most painful moments of our lives.

Honest Love Letters

Scripture was the healing ointment to my wounds. His Word brought life. I wrote lines of Scripture on post-it notes, napkins, and index cards. I wrote Scripture in my own words. I journaled responses to Scripture. I wrote and wrote and wrote it out. Soaking in Scripture helped me ride the waves of hell's advances.

Don't misunderstand, my Scripture writing and journaling didn't look like peaceful early mornings spent with my Bible and a cup of coffee, tucked cozily under a blanket. No, this was the most honest prayer of my life. This kind of Scripture writing looked like tear-soaked pages with deep ridges from the pressure of my angry pen. I didn't recite Scripture with a smile on my face, but while sobbing in a puddle on the floor of my shower.

Even our Savior cried out in His mental anguish on the cross. His glory was found in His surrender despite the cost. Our glory is found in the same.

His glory was found in His surrender despite the cost. Our glory is found in the same.

Let Us Pray

Lord, Your Word is an honest love letter that speaks truth to me. Your Word can turn my frown upside down and take away my anxiety. Thank You for bringing peace in the midst of my unraveling. Thank you for being my Water in the middle of the desert. Thank you for bringing joy into my moments of mess and confusion. Thank You for using me although I am unqualified. Thank You for using the "boot camp" moments to teach me. You refine me and You smooth my rough edges as You unravel me. Thank You for walking by side and for giving me the assurance of Your Word. Amen.

Chapter 25

WALKING AWAY, OR WALKING TOWARD?

In May of 2018, God asked me to walk away from my real estate business. But long before that—long before I even entered real estate—I experienced a different unraveling.

In 2012, my marriage was in shambles. We had just moved from Texas to Nashville. I left an amazing job and community of friends for a job that turned out to be…not as great as I expected. Cort closed his own law firm in Texas, and upon arriving in Nashville, discovered that he was two weeks too late to take the BAR and get licensed in Tennessee. We were both deeply disappointed and frustrated by our circumstances. The stress took a toll on our marriage, and we both felt it. We both desperately needed God to touch us and heal us.

Finally, we decided that something had to give in order to save our marriage. We decided that I needed to quit my job. Although the job wasn't as great as I expected, understand that leaving the workforce was a major blow to my identity. I was used to working, and I was good at what I did. Now, I was about to be a full-time mom.

A few months into the stay-at-home gig, I was depressed. I felt like I had no place in the world. I no longer knew who I was. Nothing about this season felt good. I felt like I was dying inside. I lost everything I knew to be true. I was being tormented day and night. I would drop my kids off at school with a smile, then come home and crawl into bed, slipping between the sheets of depression and anxiety.

Eventually, I decided to place my pain in God's hands. So every day, I dragged my patio chair to the end of our backyard and stared out over the green pasture behind our house. I would cry, and I would pray.

191

Psalm 23 rushed over my aching heart.

"The Lord is my shepherd, I shall not want. He makes me lie down in green pastures.

He restored my soul. He guides me in paths of righteousness for His name's sake.
Even though I walk through the valley of the shadow of death, I will fear no evil.
For you are with me. Your rod and your staff, they comforted me." –Psalm 23:1-4

I longed for running waters of joy, but all I felt was sorrow. But day after day, the Lord brought me back to this psalm. It became God's promise to me. He would restore my soul. He would give me rest. Even though I felt death creeping in and hell raging against me, I chose to believe that God was with me and that He would deliver me.

"You prepare a table for me in the presence of my enemies. You anoint my head
with oil; my cup overflows. Surely goodness and love will follow me all the days of
my life, and I will dwell in the house of the Lord forever." –Psalm 23:5-6

I allowed Psalm 23 to seep into my every cell. I faithfully met God in that pasture, day after day. One day, He spoke His plans into my heart.

"Tiffany, real estate is part of your healing. Go get your real estate license."

His goodness and kindness followed me the entire time I worked in real estate.

Not What Lies Behind, But What Lies Ahead

Paul was in awe of God's master plan. God was able to take the prime persecutor of Christians and turn him into a Christian-making machine.

Paul often wrote about his hardships and how we, as Christians, should not be surprised when hardship comes our way. While some may believe suffering and pain equates to God's abandonment, Paul didn't see it that way at all. He believed in the revolution of the faith.

When we walk in agreement with Jesus, as Paul did, we overthrow Satan's plans. We place ourselves in the camp of victory. When we sign up to join God's revolution for our lives, we sign up to choose joy even in the unraveling. We choose to sing praises of delight even during our disappointments. We walk away from our former ways—even if they were good ways—in order to walk more closely with God's plan. When we do this, all of hell trembles as we leave our past behind and walk toward God's eternal glory.

"And the God of all grace, who called you to his eternal glory in Christ after you have suffered a little while, will himself restore you and make you strong, firm, and steadfast." –1 Peter 5:10

We don't unravel alone! Christ is always with us. We can't turn from our emotions and choose lasting joy without His grace, and He is oh-so-willing to give it. So rest in Him during the process. When you believe you aren't good enough or strong enough, rest in Him. When you grow impatient for His plan to be revealed, rest in Him. When you feel exhausted and defeated, rest in Him. God knows that the principal of pain produces gain, and He is with you through it all.

"I waited patiently for the Lord; he turned to me and heard my cry. He lifted me out of the slimy pit, out of the mud and mire; he set my feet on a rock and gave me a firm place to stand. He put a new song in my mouth, a hymn of praise to

our God. Many see and fear and put their trust in the Lord. Blessed is the man who makes the Lord his trust who does not look proud."-Psalm 40:1-3

God might be calling you to walk away from something comfortable. He might be ready to shake you out of your complacency. Trust me, I know the fear. I know the hesitation and the excuses. But I can promise you that when you follow His call and trust Him completely, He won't lead you to desolation. He will lead you to verdant pastures.

Let Us Pray

Lord, I know that what I feel and see right now isn't the end game. I might feel surrounded by despair and darkness, but You, Holy Ghost, lead me through with Your light. Lord, You are faithful and loyal. You never give up on me and no one can remove Your promises from my life. Even now, You are refreshing my soul. My fears are falling and my heart is being renewed. While everything in my life might be shifting, You never change. Help me to walk in the uncomfortable. Unravel my mindsets and comfortable patterns. Help me walk in confidence, knowing Who I serve. Amen!

Part Six

THE PURPOSE AND THE REVEAL

You've made it this far. You've come to the part where your persistence pays off in God's glory. It would have been easier for you to take the wide road, the easy way, the shortcut. But you've gone all-in like Abraham, Moses, David, Isaiah, Elizabeth, Peter, and Jesus Himself. You've realized that, because you were created with a specific, divine purpose, you must first position yourself to receive the unraveling. You've embraced the truth that only in this will you be molded into the image of Christ.

"Many are the plans in a man's heart, but it is the Lord's purpose that prevails."
—Proverbs 19:21

"The one who calls you is faithful and He will do it."—1 Thessalonians 5:24

The reveal in the process of unraveling is all about accepting the Lord's purpose and allowing His way to rule. It's about embracing our story, not allowing shame to hold it captive. Through the unraveling process, God reveals our character and our story so that the lives of others can be touched by ours.

How many times have you gotten stuck on the question of God's will? We ask, "Lord, what is Your perfect plan for my life? When will You reveal it?" Then, we live our lives in fear. We feel like we might miss it, so we become paralyzed and stagnant instead of taking each little step forward.

I am convinced that God's will for each of us isn't the big final moment, or something He flashes brightly. I believe His will is discovered through the unraveling process. It is found in the tearing down and building up. With

195

each day, God reveals another step. He lays another brick, building the house of our heart more firmly on the foundation of His love.

Productive Pain

When we approach God's Word with confidence and expect Him to speak to us directly, we invite Him to speak specific truth to our hearts. We open ourselves to His life-changing voice.

During one season of unraveling, the Lord said to me, "Tiffany, my kingdom is not a matter of talk, but of power. What do you prefer? Shall I come to you with a whip, or in love with a gentle spirit?"

When we finally stop fighting and look up, we adopt God's perspective.

While we're in pain, it can feel like God comes to us with a whip. His ways can feel harsh. We might feel like our unraveling is cruel. But the wisdom found in Scripture shows us that change and testimony come from our sufferings. Our unraveling brings lasting change and true peace. When we finally stop fighting and look up, we adopt God's perspective. We listen to His voice as we discern which way to move until we see His purpose clearly. This beautiful moment is the reveal.

Before we dive into this final section, I'd like for you to take some time to write your two-minute story.

Choose an unraveling that stands out in your heart and mind. Maybe it's the one you're walking through right now. Start from the beginning. Use what we have learned in this book. Put into the words the hardship you have faced and how it has made you who you are today.

How did this particular unraveling impact you, positively and negatively? How did you come to the point of clinging to God and walking the narrow way? How did you choose joy in the midst of your sorrow? What truth in His Word carried you through this unraveling?

God has written a story that is unique to you so that when people hear your story, they can be amazed anew by His power. Our stories are important. God uses our stories as an avenue for His freeing truth. Through our stories, He delivers His love and grace to others so that they will hold fast to Him as they walk through their own unraveling processes. Together, as God's people, we can help each other become more whole in Christ.

Let Us Pray

Lord, help me to see that my story is the finest thing in life. It takes time to unfold. You build it by setting one brick at a time. Thank You for being the Craftsman. Give me the courage, faith, and conviction to share my story. Amen!

Chapter 26

AWARE OF MY FLAWS

How many times have you stared at yourself in the mirror, desperate to change yourself? Maybe it's your looks, but maybe you see deeper and wish to change your heart. We are our biggest critics, and no one knows us better than we know ourselves.

But in the unraveling process, coming to grips with our flaws isn't a bad thing. Our flaws make us more dependent on Christ, and that's true freedom. When we allow God to unravel us, our dialogue shifts from, "Why, Lord?" to, "Wow, Lord!"

As we've journeyed through unraveling to believe, we've allowed God to teach us to trust through prayer and to develop our spiritual palates. We've unraveled our comfortable patterns, and we've learned how to choose joy in the midst of our suffering.

Now, we will look at how our good God turns our flaws into beauty.

Paul's Honesty

The further Paul ventured in life and ministry, the more he became aware of his flaws. He gained a deep understanding of how much he depended on God as life's hardships unraveled him. Paul referred to himself as the "least of the apostles" (1 Corinthians 15:9) and "the chief of all sinners" (1 Timothy 1:15).

Paul wasn't speaking negatively of himself. He didn't have self-esteem issues. Paul had simply come to see the unraveling process for what it was. He saw that when he came to the end of himself, the Lord was there, ready to make him into a new creation. Paul endured stoning and imprisonment, yet his hope and faith in Christ stood firm. He relied on God completely.

God offers us the same grace today. The same grace that strengthened and sustained Paul is given to us.

This world will undoubtedly do everything it can to break us. But we have to breathe deeply, knowing that even our flaws will be used for God's glory. What the world sees as weakness, God will reveal as strength.

What the world sees as weakness, God will reveal as strength.

Let's return to Romans 8:28. In fact, let's write it down:

"And we know that in all things God works for the good of those who love him, who have been called according to his purpose."

Speak this truth over your life and your flaws! Allow God to do the second part of this unraveling process; allow Him to remake you.

Handing on What We've Lived

Think about the unraveling you're walking through right now. Are you able to see ways that God will use those to transform your heart and to show forth His glory? Write those ways below.

Paul gave great advice to Timothy, his son in the faith, in order to renew him. Paul knew that Timothy would experience his own unraveling. He wanted to give Timothy some truth to cling to and to offer some solidarity. I like to think he offers us the same advice for our own unraveling.

> *"Timothy, my son, I am giving you this command in keeping with the prophecies once made about you, so that by recalling them you may fight the battle well, holding on to faith and a good conscience, which some have rejected and so have suffered shipwreck with regard to the faith."* –1 Timothy 1:18-19

In what situation are you fighting the good fight?

How are you clinging to God's truth?

In the space below, journal a prayer offering your flaws to the Father. Let Him into the most tender areas of your heart. Ask Him to use even your flaws for His glory.

Let Us Pray

Lord, help me fight the good fight. Help me to stand on Your Word. Help me realize that this world isn't my home. Build my confidence in You and Your victory. Seal me in Your blood, Jesus. Let it be done in Your Name! Amen!

Chapter 27

GOD'S GLORY

As I sat in the waiting room of the dentist's office, my anxiety increased. I detest coming to the dentist. My daughter, Kailee, who happens to love the dentist, came with me, even making sure we arrived 15 minutes early.

Our seats in the waiting room were the closest ones to the door. I could hear *everything*. The suctioning. The drills. I tried to block out the noise. That lasted about five minutes. I couldn't stop fidgeting. I was in a near panic. I looked at my daughter and said, "I have to go wait in the car. I can't do this." I informed the ladies at the front desk and booked it straight to my car.

In my car with the air blasting, my breath finally started to slow. I gave myself a pep talk and reminded myself that sometimes good things require discomfort. I know that taking care of my teeth is a good thing, a worthy effort, but it does take effort. And pain. And lots of laughing gas.

We tend 203ot he203k that if someone really loves us, they will never ask us to do what is uncomfortable. We forget that hardship is a road to healing. 203ot he, an illness, tragic car accident, unplanned pregnancy, debt, and betrayal all led to God's glory being lived in my life. It doesn't make sense 203ot he world. But neither did the cross.

The Symbol of Our Victory

The power and glory of God is summarized in the symbol of the cross. The cross symbolizes death and new life. What seemed to be a defeat ushered in a great victory. This power of God delivers, overcomes, and transforms.

Nothing beats the power and the glory of the cross, not even the most impossible situations. The cross gets the final word. Every time.

Maybe you're struggling to believe in the power of the cross. Maybe you doubt your worthiness to receive the glory of the cross. None of us are worthy. But there is no place or circumstance that cannot be touched by God's glory. You are never out of reach!

If God will reach into a filthy high school bathroom and lift a pregnant teenager off the floor, He will reach into your life as well. While the unraveling might not be pretty, allow the cross to have the final word in your life.

Think about a current situation in which you need to thank God specifically for what He has done and for how He has come through for you. Keep in mind, God's final answers aren't always what we expect them to be. Sometimes we want a "yes" and God says, "Not yet."

How has God used a cross in your life to wipe away sin and bring about new life in you?

How do you think your story glorifies God? Are you regularly sharing your story? If not, what's holding you back?

"They triumphed over him by the blood of the Lamb and by the word of their testimony; they did not love their lives so much as to shrink from death." —Revelation 12:11

Rewrite this verse in your own words:

Let Us Pray

Lord, help me take the discomforts of life and learn that even they can refine my flaws. Holy Spirit, remind me that You bring beauty from the ashes. Give me courage to share my story, even when it's not fully written. Bless my testimony so that it brings You glory. Amen

Chapter 28

IDENTITY

What happens when everything we know to be true falls apart? When people who are supposed to protect us betray or abandon us? What happens when God doesn't restore order or love?

When we find ourselves in a mess like this, our only option is to re-form our identities in Christ. Will we choose to identify our lives with God? Or will we walk away from Him, heartbroken and with an illusion of control?

Once we start looking for God in every area of our lives, we will find Him easily. But we have to look for Him in *every* part, even those areas we hope no one ever discovers. In these areas, God whispers new truths and invites us to exchange our old beliefs for an identity rooted in Him.

Jeremiah, a prophet of the Old Testament, lived during one of Israel's most troubled times. When we first meet Jeremiah, it is a decade before the fall of Jerusalem in 587 BC, which was followed by the Babylonian exile. To say that the Israelites were about to have a major identity crisis is an understatement. All hell was about to break loose for God's chosen people. Families would be ripped apart, children enslaved, and many people killed. When God called Jeremiah, the Israelites were already starting to unravel. Things already looked desperate. So God chose Jeremiah to deliver a difficult message of truth.

If there was ever a man who showed grit in the midst of mental and physical exhaustion, it was Jeremiah. He was rejected because of the messages he delivered. He was persecuted and doubted. Yet he allowed God to refine his character so that he wouldn't back down, even in the face of such hostility. He found his identity in God alone, not in what he did or what other people thought of him.

Baby, You're a Diamond

In December 2018, I was completely broken. It was less than a week before Christmas, and I hadn't done any shopping. Depression had seized my heart, and I was fighting back with all I had. But the fight left me feeling depleted and unable to give as much as I wanted. I tried to reserve all my energy and cheer for my children, but it's tough to be jolly when all you feel is heaviness.

I was in the middle of a toy aisle in the store, trying to find the perfect present for my niece. I was overwhelmed by everything: the toys, the choices, the disappointment, the guilt. I sat down in the middle of the aisle, put my head between my knees, and wept as people stepped around me.

I knew the root of my sadness. When I walked away from my business, I lost a piece of my identity. I knew it wasn't good to place my identity in anything other than God, but I was proud of what I built. It became so easy to receive all my worth from titles and accolades. In this moment, I knew Jesus wanted to heal these disordered parts of my heart and help me find my true identity in Him. But that required me to smash my pride and to allow myself to be reformed.

This is the ultimate purpose of the unraveling process. The unraveling process consists of the baby steps we need to deeply understand how God identifies us. And don't worry about whether or not God really knows or cares about your identity.

"For you created my inmost being, you knit me together in my mother's womb."
—Psalm 139:13

He knew us before we even existed. He dreamt us up! Every last detail about us is thought of and known by our Creator. He gave us very specific personalities, natural strengths, and preferences. He knows us better than we know ourselves.

Some of our greatest strengths and characteristics don't surface until pressure is applied during the unraveling process. But if we cling to God as we wrestle through the hardship, He will reveal the very best parts of us.

What are some of your God-revealing characteristics that have been revealed to you during your most difficult times?

How has your personality and character helped you stick it out through troublesome times?

A Heart Remodel

In the very first chapter of Jeremiah, God revealed that He would have to do some tearing out and replanting. Some of us might need to experience a similar exchange. We need to exchange our old way of thinking for God's truth. During this unraveling-to-reveal process, God doesn't leave us. He doesn't change His mind about us or grow weary of us. He is always teaching us about His love and equipping us to tell our stories. The tearing down might be painful, but our heavenly Contractor is right there, at every moment, making plans for our remodel.

Take a moment and think about a time when you felt God very close to you.

Now, think about the wilderness moments. Those times when you intensely felt the destruction of your false identity. How did you see God's hand moving even then?

God's rebuilding is our reveal. We can't tell our stories if we don't know who we are. This is the final piece of the unraveling process.

Below is part of a prayer I journaled during my identity crisis. Feel free to make it your own prayer if you're in the middle of being rebuilt more firmly in Jesus.

Lord, terror and pain are stalking me. Lies and manipulation are stalling me while truth is trying to break through and move in. I pray. I call. And yet nothing. Why are you silent? Climbing towards You, I remain. One foot in front of the other on this… My faith is shaking yet I remain. I smile, I cry all the while…

Despite my heaviness God, You never leave. My identity is hidden deep inside and yet into the refiner's fire You send me. Burning off the mess to make me the diamond of Your design…

Noah waited 120 years and endured rejection, ridiculed for his promise. Abraham and Sarah waited 25 years. Joseph, enslaved and betrayed, waited 13 years. All the while You remained with them and reformed them according to Your glorious plans. Do the same for me.

Where I see brokenness, God sees beauty. And while most of us want a quick fix for our unraveling (I know I do!), remember, God plays the long game. The unraveling and the reveal take time. But, oh, how worth it it is in the end.

Habit vs. Identity

An important distinction to make here is that of habit vs. identity. It's a fine line. We have to look closely to see the difference. But it's vital.

Often, many of us tend to associate our identities with our habits. Others even describe or identify us based on our habits, whether they are good or bad. This is where the notion of labels comes into play. But we know that God is bigger than labels and greater than habits!

Forming good habits or breaking bad ones comes down to our decisions and actions. We decided to do or not do something, and then we act. Habit formation is dependent upon what we choose and how much we're willing to work toward the formation or destruction of that habit.

While we can form or break our habits, we cannot form or break our identities in Christ. There's nothing we can do to be made *more* in God's image. We just are! Fully and completely. And there's nothing we can do to break from our true identities in God. My identity does not lie in my habits. While I can choose whether or not to see my identity in Him, there's nothing I can do to change that truth.

So don't let the enemy fool you into thinking that you can earn or lose your identity. Remember, you get to choose how you see yourself. Just like God led Jeremiah to see his full self in God, He invites us to shed our false ideals and embrace our true identities in Him.

What lie do you to need exchange about yourself for God's truth about who you are in Him?

In what ways do you feel "not good enough"? Have others insinuated this? How so? And how have you believed their words over the Word of the Lord?

Let Us Pray

Lord, show me my true identity. Help me to break any bad habits and form only good habits according to Your call on my life. Lord, in moments when I doubt my goodness found in You, open my eyes to see the truth. Help me to trust in Your love and Your perfect design. Jesus, when I look in the mirror and see things I don't like about myself, remind me that I am beautiful in Your sight. When I look in my heart and see things I don't like, remind me that You created me to be good. I want to find my identity in You, and You alone. Let it be, in Jesus' Name! Amen.

Chapter 29

PRODUCE HOPE

Early one morning, Cort and I were woken up by a phone call. That's the kind of call that gets your blood racing before you even answer.

Unfortunately, it was bad news. Heartbreaking news. The home that my husband grew up in—the one his parents still lived in—was struck by lightening during the night. The lightening ignited a massive fire. Thankfully, Cort's parents were able to get out and save a few important items. But what a devastation it was for Cort, his parents, and his siblings! They lost sentimental items and their childhood home without the chance to say goodbye.

The fire chief discovered that the location of the lightening strike was near several containers of gas kept in the garage for their lawn mower. Hearing that news brought us to our knees even more. While in our sorrow, we were able to give thanks for God's deliverance. There was a wall of protection there that night, and because of it, we still had Cort's parents to hug.

When his parents returned to the house to survey the damage, they painted the phrase "Beauty from Ashes" on their garage. What a beautiful example of hope amidst sorrow they gave us!

The Root and the Reveal are God's Love

All of our lives are filled with these crazy moments. But if we're willing to see them, the details of these moments reveal hope found in God. God gives Himself to us fully, and He never leaves our side during our unraveling. When we feel abandoned, God runs after us. When we feel weak, God carries us. When we doubt, God sends His Holy Spirit to inspire and encourage us.

The world tries to conform us, but Jesus desires to transform us. He wants to tell a fuller story with our lives. He wants to reveal how passionate His love for us really is, and how far He is willing to go to reach us. Jesus is not bound by our sins or shortcomings. He sees far outside our labels and patterns.

Many times, when God drops a promise or a dream into our hearts, we want to get past the process and live the dream. But really, He needs us to slow down, accept the silence, and grow comfortable in the waiting. There's no easy button with God because there's no real glory in immediacy. Our stories are built upon our mess, our unraveling, and our discovery of self in the heart of God.

We deserve total destruction for our sins. Instead, God, in His splendor, wisdom, and mercy, pours out heaven's love for you and for me. All we have to do to accept this gift is to utter, "Jesus, I'm a sinner. Help me! I need You!" He extended His mercy to those who feared Him, hated Him, and rejected Him. He could forsake us without any regret, but His love compels Him to do otherwise. What a good God we have!

"For God so loved the world that He sent his only son that whosoever believe in Him shall not perish, but have everlasting life." –John 3:16

Jesus was never ashamed of the "old Tiffany." There was nothing to be proud about in the old me, and yet Jesus chose me. He produced hope in me and sustained me during each unraveling. And He'll continue to do so when I unravel again. He brings me life with His Word. He bore my shame and covered me with His protection. He planted dreams where there was despair and healing where there was brokenness. Anytime I wanted to veer from Him, He gently called me back to His love, His mercy, and His promise. When life scattered my hope, God never worried. He knew what He was doing. He was rebuilding me. He was preparing me.

God Has Chosen You

If the stories from Scripture discussed in this book haven't convinced you, let me repeat it to you here: God chooses the down-and-out people, the people with the junk, the people who are "lost causes." He meets them where they are, in the middle of hopelessness, and He shows them what true hope looks like. Through His grace and love, He unravels and rebuilds them.

He does the same with us! God gives us hope when all seems lost! We have to really, truly walk in this hope. We have to unleash this hope for others so that they can hear the life-changing message of the cross. Hope is the ember that sparks the fire. And once it spreads, it's impossible to ignore. It's the lightening strike that compels us to find beauty amongst the ashes!

Will you let God produce this kind of hope in you? Will you be willing to share it with others?

Let Us Pray

God, I praise You for choosing me, even with all my mess and junk. Thank You for giving me hope when all seems lost. Time and time again, you use misfits, dysfunctional families, adulterers, liars, cheaters, and cowards to bring about Your glory. Lord, I am counted among the sinners, and yet You call me to Yourself. Thank You, Jesus, for bringing beauty from my ashes. May I always return to give Your praise. Amen!

Chapter 30

YOU HAVE A STORY TO TELL

Throughout your entire unraveling process, God has been patiently equipping, maturing, and developing character in you. You will look back at who you were before the unraveling and see that you now look more like Christ.

God has placed a calling on each of us to share the stories of our unraveling. Through us, God communicates His power, mercy, and love. When we speak with others about our unraveling experience—whether it's with one person or 1,000 people—we invite them into the beautiful process. This is our spiritual influence.

We've each been gifted with different stories and different unraveling moments that take place at different times. We're in different communities and we have different friends. God has orchestrated this so that His saving message can be brought to more of His children. The unraveling you've gone through? It's all a part of of the Master's plan to weave the ultimate tapestry in your life. Through God's grace, we get the choice to embrace the process and watch Him fulfill the promise. The result is an earth-shaking story of God's love.

We can encourage others simply by resting in who God made us to be. God isn't interested in you being me or me being you. Don't compare your story to mine. Unraveling can cause us to turn our heads to the left or right, but let's keep our eyes fixed straight ahead on Jesus and the work He is performing in our unique lives. We mute God's magnificent colors when we try to fabricate our unraveling. But remember, He is the Master weaver. We can't and shouldn't pick the textures and colors of His weaves.

Growing up, I was in Girl Scouts. I was never really one for the activities we participated in—I longed for adventure more than sewing and crafting.

But one particular year, my mom was the troop leader, and she was amazing. She decided that we would all earn our badges for cross stitching. She told us, "Girls, don't worry about how messy it looks on the bottom. There will be knots and crossovers. You might make some mistakes. But from the top, you will only see a beautiful masterpiece!"

To this day, her words help me better understand God's perspective on our unraveling. We see the bottom, the mess, the mistakes, the knots. So often, we can only see the thing right in front of us. But God takes the perspective from the top, seeing us as His masterpieces, eager to bless the world with our beauty.

Our stories bring life, in all their color. Our stories bring others hope and inspiration.

Our stories bring life, in all their color.

Through Him and for Him

At the beginning of our unraveling journey together, we asked some big questions. We wondered why these things happen to us, why God would allow us to walk through hard times. And we saw how God has used and continues to use desert moments to lead His chosen ones to the most wonderful lands.

Hopefully, our perspectives have shifted. Now, we see that God uses everything—even the most horrible circumstances—to bring about good in our lives and in our world. We know that God unravels us so that we can come to the end of ourselves and come more fully to Him. We don't have to know it all or hold it all together. We've come to the point of total surrender and trust. Real trust. Honest, crying-in-the-shower trust. We've removed the comfortable patterns in our lives that were really distractions from God and stumbling blocks along our way.

Now, we understand that unraveling isn't a sign of weakness. It's not necessarily a punishment. Unraveling is beautiful! When we allow ourselves to be unraveled, we place ourselves in the arms of Jesus. We find joy, even when we're sorrowful. We hold fast to peace and promise. We know that He works all things together for our good. We don't have to have mighty faith to embrace the unraveling process, only faith the size of a mustard seed.

Let's continue to put on the armor of God and fight the good fight. Let's continue to allow Him to unravel us so that we will be more like Him. And let's tell our stories. Your story is a story to be told. A story to be shared. A story that will tell others this simple truth: God knows. He sees. He cares. He accompanies. He loves. He will use it all for your good and for His glory!

Let Us Pray

Here, write your own concluding prayer. Let it be a prayer of victory, even if you're still in battle. Let it be a prayer of praise, even if you feel depressed. Let it be a prayer of freedom, even if you are still enslaved. And let it be a prayer of surrender to Jesus, offering everything you have and everything you are to His heart and His kingdom.

Amen!

ACKNOWLEDGMENTS

Unraveled was not possible without the love and support of so many friends and family. I will never have enough time to express my gratitude. I now understand the pressure celebrities feel during their acceptance speeches at award shows!

Thank you to the following, for all their hard work through the long process of writing:

Cort, the man who has been with me, hand in hand, during all our seasons of unraveling. Thank you for always supporting my dreams and pushing me to follow Jesus, even when it wasn't easy. Thank you for picking up the burden and putting your dreams on hold so that I could go after mine. Thanks for sticking and staying when it would have been easier to walk away.

Rielly, for the grace you extended to a young teenage mom who had no clue how to parent. Thank you for encouraging me to write this book and not quit, even when others made fun of me for doing so.

Chaise, for being my encourager every morning and praying for me during our drives to school. Thank you for reminding me that fear doesn't have a place in my story. Your faithfulness to prayer and to me helped make this book possible.

Kailee Grace, for being my partner in crime at the coffee shops. Thank you for quoting Scripture to me and for putting up with me worshipping at the top of my lungs while you tried to do homework. Thank you for praying fervently over this book.

Mom and Dad, there are no words. Thank you for raising me to love God. Thank you for your love and protection. Thank you for listening to me read the first draft of this book for hours on end, believing in me every step of the way.

My little sister, Jamie, for being my biggest fan. You reminded me that I was born to write and you eased my worldly fears. I'm forever grateful for the gift of you. Makayla, thanks for letting Aunt Tiffy spend countless hours on the phone with your mom!

Ginger Bethmann, my prayer partner through so many unraveling moments. I couldn't ask for a better teacher and mother-in-law. Your spiritual mentorship and book recommendations bring me so much joy and laughter.

Jamie Harper, my unofficial editor and best friend who spent hours pouring over this book with me. Thank you for crying with me. You believed in me before I believed in myself.

Charles Harper, my brother from another mother. Thank you for your spiritual and temporal support. Thank you for your constant encouragement, even when I would cuss and cry.

April Underwood, my longest friend who loves me for me. Thanks for not kicking me to the curb after middle school.

Jennifer Wooten, for believing in me and praying over the outline and for those who would read it.

Georgetta, for your constructive feedback. I value your opinion so much.

Pastor Harry, for personally coming beside me and counseling me during my 2012 unraveling season. Thanks for always pointing me to Jesus.

Pastor Charlie, for calling me in November 2018 and sharing that God said, "Get to writing!" Thank you for sharing your wisdom, knowledge, notes, and commentaries. Thank you for challenging me to be better.

ACKNOWLEDGMENTS

Stephanie and Kevin, your belief in me and support in raising money for this book will forever mean the world to me! Thank you for feeding us during these long months. Your dinners and your prayers sustained me.

Tuesday Bible Study Ladies, led by Dixie, for giving me space to share my passion and dreams. And lots of ugly tears. You are my people.

Aunt Debbie and Uncle Mark, you have always been in my corner. Thank you for believing in me and donating to make this book a possibility.

Gram and Grampa Bethmann, for the countless prayers and endless support. This book exists because of the both of you.

Monica, Rodney, and Tessa, for coming alongside me.

Christina, for being the first lady to believe in my cause.

Olivia, for being the best editor and cheerleader I know! Thank you for partnering with me and making this a reality.

Bev and Ian, for helping me brainstorm my vision.

Pam Hall and Cana Salon, for making me look beautiful and loving on me during an unraveling season.

Bangs and Blush, for your amazing support in making me look like a hot momma for my photos!

Maggie, for putting your life on hold and spending long evenings making sure I didn't use the same word over and over. Thank you for being my author-buddy and for reminding me that even books are written step by step.

Megan, for listening to my story and encouraging me to share it!

Uncle Gene, Aunt Karen, and Corey, for coming alongside me as I unraveled as a teenager. Thank you for opening your home to a broken girl and allowing me to have the space to hear God speak to me.

Grandpa and Ginger, for walking beside us and pouring into our lives. You instilled a legacy to seek God even when life is messy. Thank you for giving me the tools and education to tackle life head on.

Uncle Dave and Aunt Sandy, for always making us laugh, for believing in us, for supporting our dreams, and for providing the best bling-bling.

Mamaw and Papaw, for spending hours on the phone with me, reminding me that you believe in me. You never let me quit a job on the farm until it was complete. The Lord used those hours of picking blackberries and weeding the garden to teach me how to stick with it and that hard work pays off. You show me what it truly looks like to love.

NOTES

Introduction | The Need for Unraveling

1. Miriam-Webster, "unravel," accessed July 12, 2019, https://www.merriam-webster.com/dictionary/unravel

2. Henry T. Blackaby, *Experiencing God -Workbook* (Nashville, TN, Lifeway Press, 2007)180

Chapter 3 | Feeling Trapped? God Will Make a Way

1. National Domestic Violence Hotline, 1-800-799-7233

Chapter 6 | Not a Cash-in-on-Your-Connection Kind of Prayer

1. Bruce Wilkinson, *The Prayer of Jabez: Breaking Through to the Blessed Life* (Colorado Springs, Multnomah Publishers, Inc., 2000), 9-92

Chapter 11 | No Compromise

1. Bible.org, "The Hunter and the Bear," accessed July 12, 2019, https://bible.org/illustration/hunter-and-bear

Chapter 18 | Running

1. J.K. Rowling, *Harry Potter and the Goblet of Fire (New York, NY, Scholastic Inc., 2000), 695*

Chapter 22 | Step by Step

1. Whitney Houston, "Step By Step," Arista, 1996.

MEET TIFFANY

Tiffany Bethmann spent many years in corporate America in the marketing and sales industry before pursuing her passion and calling as a writer and speaker. She now shares her stories of unraveling with Christ.

Tiffany resides in Tennessee with her husband and three daughters. She is active in her home church and can be picked out of a crowd thanks to her signature red lipstick.

GET IN TOUCH!

Have a community event, ladies' church retreat, or get together coming up? Tiffany can come speak to your group! Do you have a TV show, radio show, or blog? You can book Tiffany for an interview or to speak at your next event by emailing your request to:

booktiffanybethmann@gmail.com or www.tiffanybethmann.com

Follow Tiffany on Instagram: @tiffanybethmann

Follow along on Facebook: @unraveledbook

Author website: www.tiffanybethmann.com

CPSIA information can be obtained
at www.ICGtesting.com
Printed in the USA
LVHW110010140919
631068LV00002B/7/P